THE CINEMATIC ART OF

VOLUME I

FROM LAUNCH TO WARLORDS OF DRAENOR

**TITAN
BOOKS**

INTRODUCTION

"IN THE AGE OF CHAOS, TWO FACTIONS
BATTLED FOR DOMINANCE. . . .
THESE TWO FORCES COLLIDE IN A
CONTEST OF CUNNING, INTELLECT, AND
BRUTE STRENGTH, WITH THE WINNER
CLAIMING DOMINANCE OVER THE
WHOLE OF AZEROTH. WELCOME TO THE
WORLD OF WARCRAFT."

–*WARCRAFT: ORCS & HUMANS*

Long before there was *World of Warcraft*, there was *Warcraft: Orcs & Humans*, the high-fantasy, real-time strategy game released in 1994 that first introduced players to the warring factions that have battled over Azeroth ever since. The game laid the groundwork for Blizzard Entertainment's style of real-time strategy games, emphasizing characterization and storytelling to draw players into its rich and brutal world. While the game featured only one simple cinematic, its manual added to the universe with a detailed history of the humans of Stormwind and the onslaught of orcs and introduced characters that would be revisited for decades such as Medivh, Garona, and Blackhand.

The success of *Warcraft: Orcs & Humans* guaranteed its sequel, and *Warcraft II* brought with it almost eight minutes of cinematics. Though quite simple by today's standards, these pieces represented a breakthrough for Blizzard, with each cinematic acting as a story node—not only working to set the scene, as the first *Warcraft*'s cinematic did, but helping to drive the story at key moments and rewarding players for hours of dedication. In a game where the player takes a top-down, three-quarter perspective of the map, cinematics offered an opportunity to more fully immerse the player in the world of Azeroth, bringing them a bit closer to the marauding Horde and the stalwart Alliance. "What we were hoping to do was sort of flesh things out for the player—help them fill in the blanks in their minds," says Matt Samia, who worked as a 3D artist on *Warcraft II* and would later go on to direct the cinematics team at Blizzard

The artistic style of Warcraft has always been bold and exaggerated, with splashy colors and over-the-top proportions that stress oversized shoulder pads and massive weapons. Early on, these elements helped define each character when viewed from above. Faithfully translating the world of Azeroth and its heroes into a more realistic space wasn't easy. In those early days, each member of the Blizzard cinematics team was a generalist—one person might be tasked with doing an entire scene alone, starting from a storyboard. Not quite seasoned filmmakers, the team were simply passionate about pushing Warcraft's story forward, making its high-fantasy world come alive for players.

Since the team did not have much animation-studio experience, experimentation abounded. And while traditional film productions keep regimented schedules, a Warcraft cinematic was finished only when it felt right.

By *Warcraft III*'s debut in 2002, the cinematics team had settled on a style now lovingly referred to at Blizzard as "hyperrealism." The team worked to break out the illustrative, in-game character models with a higher level of detail—plus an extra, over-the-top push. The game's opening cinematic depicts the age-old battle between orcs and humans, with a tattered banner blowing in the wind as soldiers from each faction fight to the death. The characters feel familiar to anyone versed in the Warcraft series, with the quintessential human footman and the orc grunt retaining the same silhouettes as their in-game models. But just as their war rages on, a new enemy rains down from the sky. The cinematic revealed just a bit more of Warcraft's expansive world—but it would still be years before Azeroth would fully open up to players in *World of Warcraft*.

The following pages seek to give insight into the creative process of the artists and filmmakers at Blizzard who've worked to make *World of Warcraft*—with its many races, countless lands, and epic storylines—a bit more real.

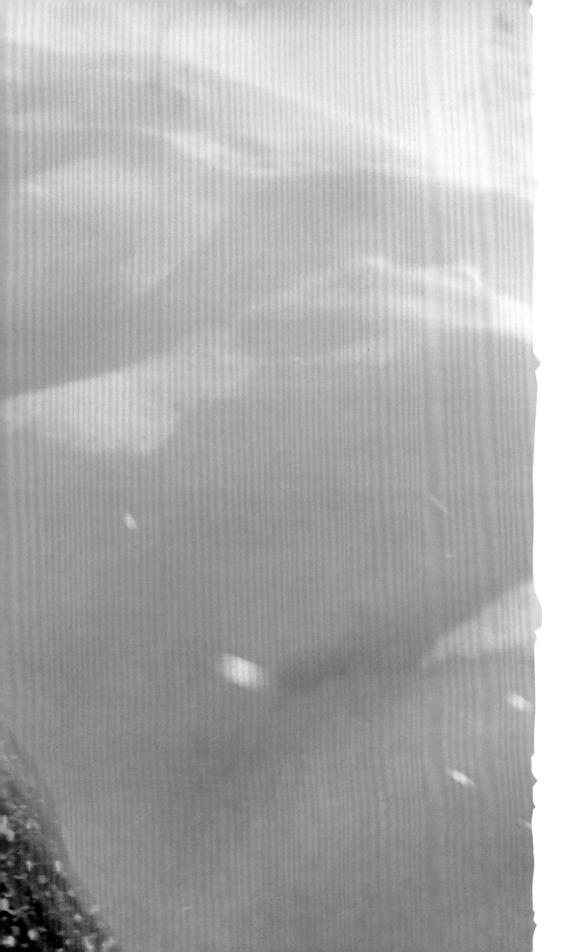

1 WORLD OF WARCRAFT

A new age was dawning on Azeroth. War with the undead Scourge and the demonic Burning Legion had left deep wounds in the world. Only the heroic efforts of the Horde, Alliance, and other defenders had spared Azeroth from destruction. But their victory did not lead to a permanent peace. Far from it. New threats soon emerged to engulf the world in conflict.

Unlike in years past, the Alliance and the Horde had many new allies to call on for help. Races like the gnomes, night elves, tauren, and Forsaken had pledged their loyalties to the factions. And from the lowest ranks of the Alliance and the Horde, a fresh generation of heroes was rising to the challenge. They came from all races, from all walks of life. Despite their differences, they shared a desire to hold back the darkness that was threatening their world.

A dwarf hunter, accompanied by his loyal bear companion, trudges up a hill in the middle of a blizzard. Snow clinging to his beard, he pauses to survey the terrain before continuing on his way, his musket doubling as a walking stick. Ironforge, the dwarves' capital, sits in the background, a city carved into the heart of a mountain. That image of the dwarf—one of the first frames of *World of Warcraft*'s inaugural cinematic—became iconic. And from that serene image, the short movie jumps to other rich locations and characters. It promises great adventure. It promises wild, open spaces full of mystery and age-old conflicts bursting back into action. Each shot represents a new corner of an unexplored world.

"The intro cinematic that came to be was born out of a desire to put the world, and not any one character or story, front and center," explains Matt Samia, who directed the cinematic: the perfect invitation for legions of players to enter the world and craft their stories—be it as a dwarf or a night elf, human or undead, tauren or orc.

THE DWARF HUNTER

SHOWING PLAYERS THAT THEY'D BE ABLE to play as a hunter—a class that can train pets to battle alongside them—seemed like an exciting way to start the cinematic. Early on, the cinematics team tested different looks for the dwarf, including an exploratory concept in full plate armor with a more modern rifle. But ultimately, the cinematics team scrapped these ideas and worked off one of the game team's hunter designs.

At the time, one of the most difficult things to accomplish in CGI was realistic hair, so the dwarf hunter, with his beard, braids, and pet bear, required a tremendous amount of time. "We had done very little hair prior to the *World of Warcraft* introduction," notes Samia. "For StarCraft's *Brood War* expansion we had done a little bit, guys in crew cuts, but very little."

The team also pulled from its work on a cinematic for the canceled *StarCraft: Ghost*. While most of the marines featured in that cinematic were bald or had close-cropped hair, Nova, the main character of the game, had a ponytail. The team also had one of the game team's developers braid his hair in the dwarven style and take headshots for reference.

ABOVE
Early concept art by the cinematics team of a dwarf in plate armor.

THE NIGHT ELF DRUID

THE CINEMATICS TEAM BEGAN WORK ON the *World of Warcraft* introduction long before many of the in-game character designs had been finalized. Originally, the game was planned to have only three playable races—humans, orcs, and tauren. For these races, the game team had already built elaborate concepts. Cinematics used these as the starting point and then worked to increase the fidelity of the models. But for other races, such as the night elf, there was much less to work off. So, the cinematics team experimented with her look, including the style of her armor, and that design formed the basis for the in-game models.

Originally, the night elf druid was destined to transform into a raven and not a panther. When the in-game ability to transform into a bird was shelved, the cinematics team reworked their plan for the scene. The team studied the movements of mountain lions, including how they use their long tails for balance, to help them animate the druid in cat form.

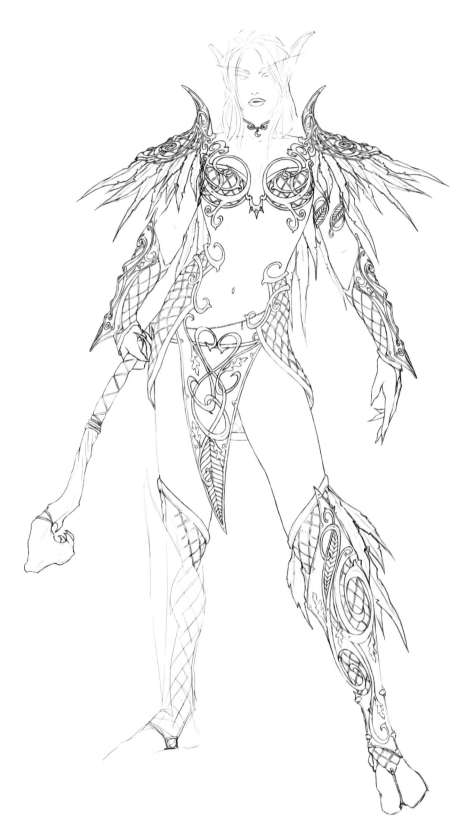

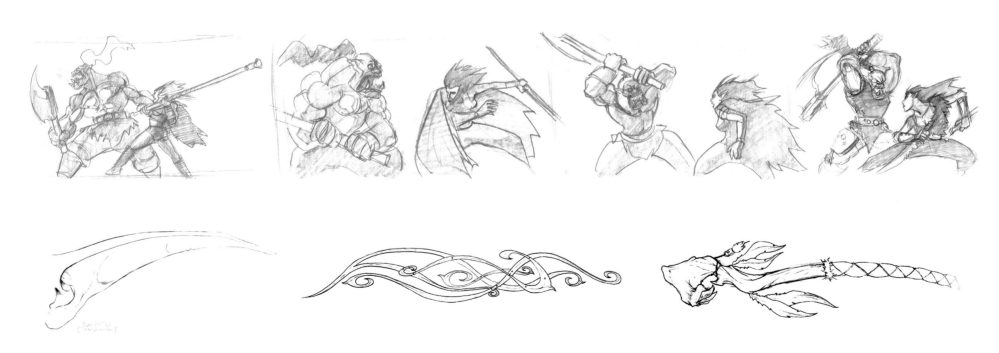

THE ORC WARRIOR

To create the cinematic's fight scenes, the team often shot video of themselves acting out the battles and used the footage as animation reference.

THE TEAM WANTED TO GIVE THE ORC warrior a commanding presence by highlighting how each of his muscles and tendons fires as he swings his club. Doing so required creating separate "morph targets" to control his musculature, each dedicated to different flexes, allowing for subtle movements across the orc's torso and neck and giving the effect that he's rippling with strength.

"THOUGH AZEROTH WAS SAVED, THE TENUOUS PACT BETWEEN THE HORDE AND THE ALLIANCE HAS ALL BUT EVAPORATED. THE DRUMS OF WAR THUNDER ONCE AGAIN."

—*WORLD OF WARCRAFT* INTRODUCTORY CINEMATIC

THE TAUREN SHAMAN

"THIS IS PROBABLY ONE OF MY FAVORITE SHOTS WE'VE DONE—AND ONE OF THE BEST-LOOKING TAUREN WE'VE EVER DONE. BUT ORIGINALLY . . . IT LOOKED LIKE A COW-MAN. IT TOOK A LOT OF WORK TO MAKE A REALISTIC TAUREN."

—SAM DIDIER, WORLD CONTENT ARTIST, *WORLD OF WARCRAFT*

In one of the last frames of the cinematic, the tauren shaman slams his totem into the ground—an ability referred to by the team as a "totem stomp." While early iterations of the game contained that ability, it was ultimately cut before release.

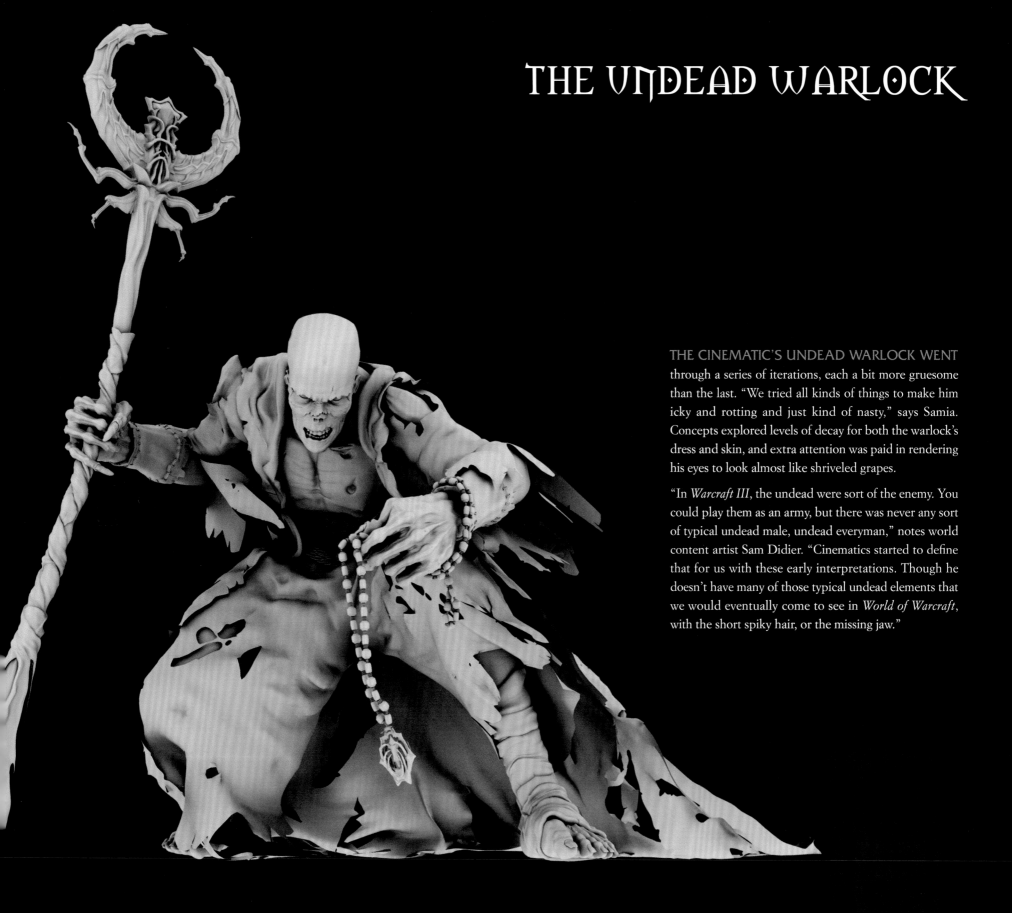

THE UNDEAD WARLOCK

THE CINEMATIC'S UNDEAD WARLOCK WENT through a series of iterations, each a bit more gruesome than the last. "We tried all kinds of things to make him icky and rotting and just kind of nasty," says Samia. Concepts explored levels of decay for both the warlock's dress and skin, and extra attention was paid in rendering his eyes to look almost like shriveled grapes.

"In *Warcraft III*, the undead were sort of the enemy. You could play them as an army, but there was never any sort of typical undead male, undead everyman," notes world content artist Sam Didier. "Cinematics started to define that for us with these early interpretations. Though he doesn't have many of those typical undead elements that we would eventually come to see in *World of Warcraft*, with the short spiky hair, or the missing jaw."

OPPOSITE AND ABOVE
The undead warlock, from untextured render to cinematic.

RIGHT
Early concept art shows the warlock with stringy red hair, red eyes, and an inlaid gem in his staff.

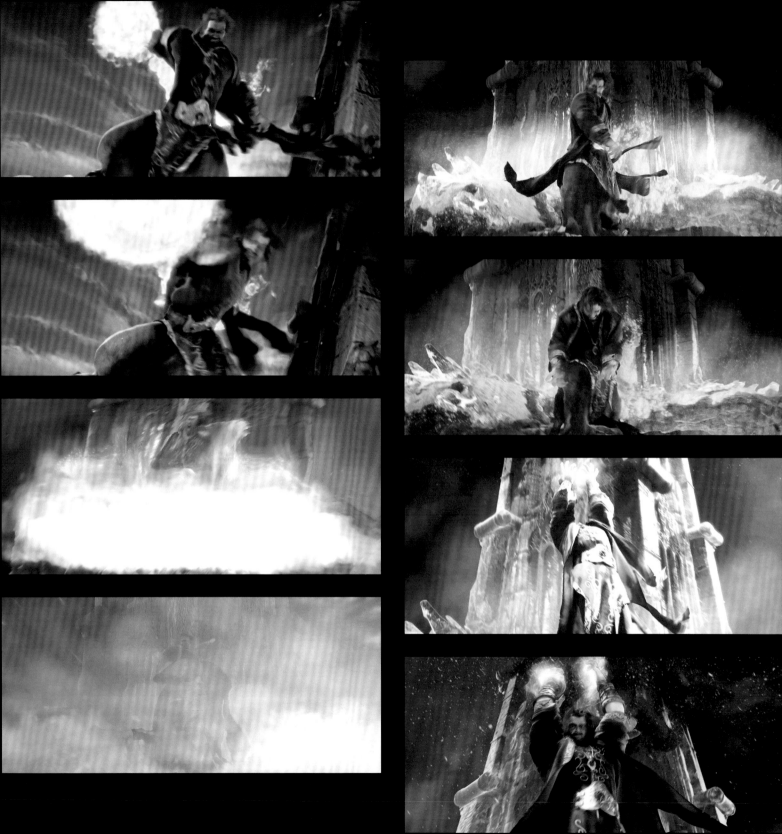

THE HUMAN MAGE

WHEN WORK BEGAN ON THE INTRODUCTORY cinematic, the game team only had a couple *World of Warcraft* models for what a human would look like. There was a human peasant with a mustache and his hair slicked back, and there were a few models that resembled knights. The cinematic's human mage, hurling fireballs down from his tower, revealed how a human would appear in *World of Warcraft*.

Concept art for the mage, who hurls down fireballs from a burning tower in the cinematic.

ENVIRONMENTS

"FOR THE FIRST *WORLD OF WARCRAFT* CINEMATIC, EVERYTHING WE DID WAS KIND OF DONE THE HARD WAY. THERE WERE NO AUTOMATED PROCESSES. WE WEREN'T REALLY USING MANY MATTE PAINTINGS. EVERY TIME WE HAD A SET, WE HAD TO HAND-BUILD EVERYTHING."

—JAMES MCCOY, CINEMATIC ARTIST

When the first cinematic was being created, the cinematics team was small and tight-knit, and it wasn't uncommon for one person to be in charge of a scene from start to finish, from concept development to building the sets and animating characters.

Environment paintings helped plan out the builds of each set and make sure each scene provided a contrast to the next.

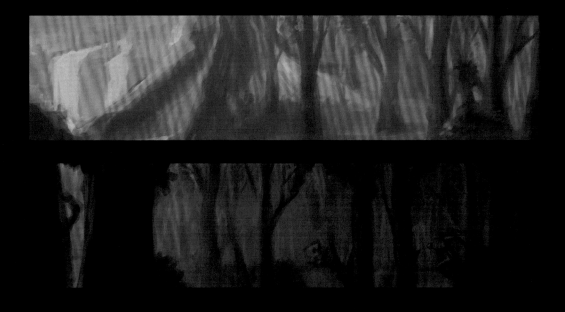

2
THE BURNING CRUSADE

For years, the Horde and the Alliance had ignored the shattered realm of Outland. The Dark Portal that linked it to Azeroth was closed. Outland was a distant threat . . .

That was, until the Dark Portal mysteriously flared back to life. The infamous demon hunter Illidan Stormrage had wrested control of Outland, and he was forging an army for unknown purposes. Elsewhere, the Burning Legion had carved out its own corner of the realm to use as a staging ground for future invasions of Azeroth.

The Horde and the Alliance could no longer ignore Outland. Aided by new allies from the ancient blood elves and the stalwart draenei, they mobilized their armies and marched through the Dark Portal. What they encountered on the other side was far worse—and far more dangerous—than they had ever expected.

"IMPRISONED FOR TEN THOUSAND YEARS.
BANISHED FROM MY OWN HOMELAND.
AND NOW YOU DARE ENTER *MY* REALM?
YOU ARE NOT PREPARED."

—ILLIDAN STORMRAGE

By the time *World of Warcraft*'s first expansion, *The Burning Crusade*, was released in January 2007, many players had explored every zone and dungeon the game had to offer. But the *Burning Crusade* expansion offered a new realm, Outland, a shattered land long cut off from Azeroth where great perils awaited. There, players would encounter lands and creatures unlike anything they had ever seen. The opening cinematic aimed to showcase what was to come and issue a challenge to the most confident and practiced of players: You are not prepared.

"That's how Illidan's line came about," notes Jeff Chamberlain, director of the cinematic. "It was a line directed straight at the players."

For the draenei character and his environment, many of the color choices were decided with the intention of creating an immediate thematic connection for viewers between this new race and the Alliance.

The design for the draenei armor developed by the cinematics team was later simplified for use in-game.

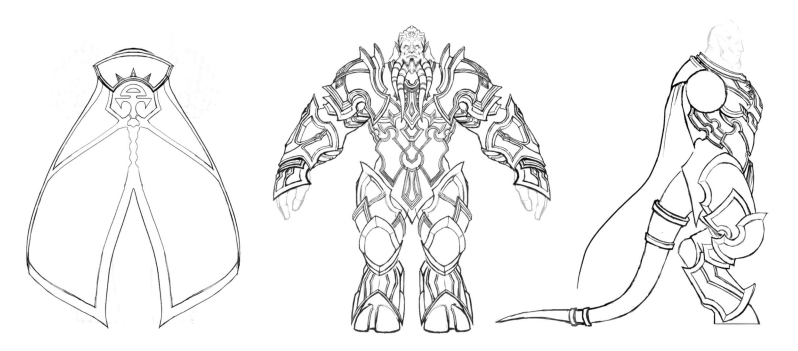

DRAENEI

TWO NEW RACES BECAME AVAILABLE TO players with *The Burning Crusade*: the draenei for the Alliance and the blood elves for the Horde. The cinematics team sought to convey the essence of these new races in ways that contrasted with the traditional ways of thinking about the Horde and the Alliance. The draenei is introduced in shadow. At first, we only see his blue eyes glowing in the dark, lending an air of mystery and menace. But as he steps into the light, he's revealed to be a righteous defender—a paladin. Every detail in the scene hints at the visual themes and culture of the draenei. Beautifully crafted archways and enchanted crystals surround the paladin, showing that his people are advanced artisans. The character's gleaming armor and use of a magic tome reveal that the draenei are an ancient race with knowledge of warfare, magic, and scholarly pursuits.

THE CINEMATIC ART OF **WORLD OF WARCRAFT**

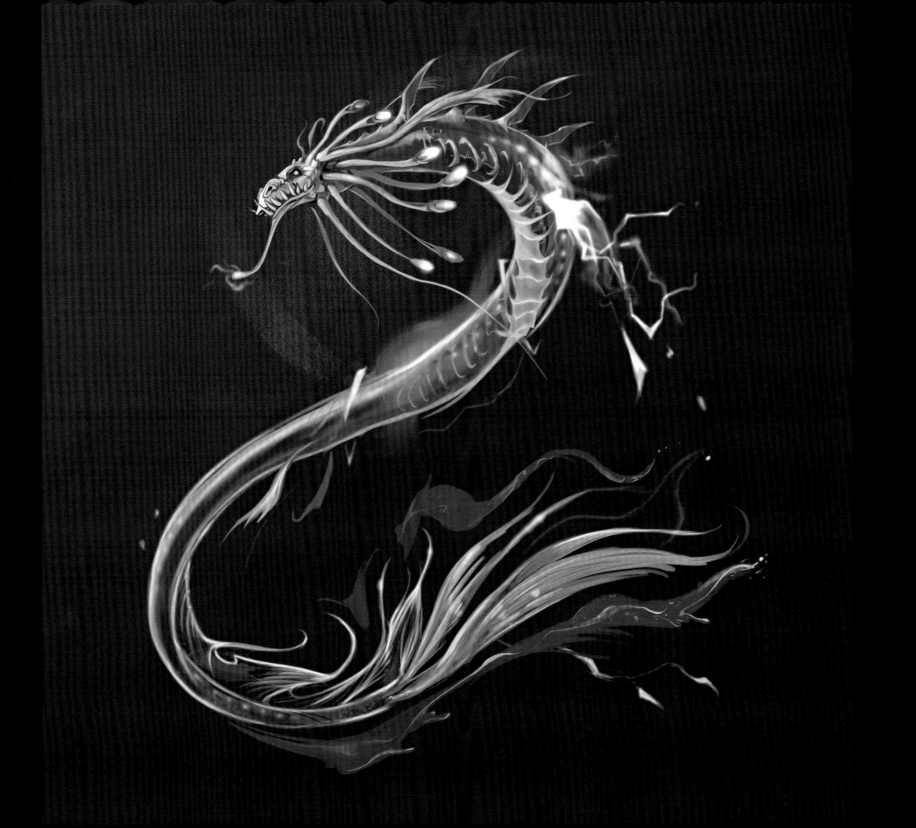

ENVIRONMENTS

MANY OF THE BACKGROUNDS IN THE
Burning Crusade cinematic are hand-drawn matte paintings rather than fully rendered 3D sets. The result is that the team had much more control over the details in the background, at the expense of some depth. In depicting the zones and locations of this new cinematic, the artists pushed color. Once you pass through the swirling fog and blowing sand and enter through the Dark Portal, the world that greets you abounds with fiery reds, vibrant greens, and deep hues of purple. Only the Swamp of Sorrows matte painting stands out for its drearier color palette—planned as a contrast for when the warlock in the film incinerates a trail of murlocs.

Outland is a shattered world. Many of its regions are harsh and desolate. The lush area of Nagrand is an exception—it was left relatively intact after the destruction of the world.

"THERE'S A LOT OF MUTUAL RESPECT BETWEEN the game team and the cinematics team," notes Chris Robinson, lead character designer for *The Burning Crusade*. "When we come to approach a new concept, or a new idea or a new expansion, there's sort of a free-for-all where people are calling out, 'Hey, we'd love to take a crack at that concept first.' Our artists end up inspiring each other. Our in-game artists want to push things as far as they can to continually develop the fidelity of the game, so they'll look to the cinematics and try to see just how much detail they can retain before it just doesn't fit, and the cinematic artists often start their work using in-game models."

"WITH *BURNING CRUSADE*, WE WERE REALLY NERVOUS ABOUT PULLING EVERYONE OUT OF THIS CORE FANTASY WORLD OF AZEROTH AND PUTTING THEM IN THIS SCI-FI ENVIRONMENT. BUT WHAT I FEEL LIKE ACTUALLY HAPPENED IS THAT THE PLAYER BASE REALLY APPRECIATED THE CHANGE, AND IT'S ALLOWED US TO NOT ALWAYS DO WHAT'S EXPECTED."

—CHRIS ROBINSON, LEAD CHARACTER DESIGNER, *THE BURNING CRUSADE*

RECURRING CHARACTERS

THE MAGE SEEN SHEEPING A TAUREN WAS intentionally based off the same model as the one hurling fireballs down from his tower in the first *World of Warcraft* cinematic. "We wanted him to have lived a bit, to have been through some adventures in this world," says Matt Samia, executive producer on the cinematic. "This is the same mage as before, but now he's got way cooler junk. He's also got a haircut for a reason we can't quite explain."

The undead warlock was also based on the character seen in the original cinematic. Like the human mage, he wears better armor and wields new abilities—a nod to how players have become more powerful and upgraded their gear over the course of playing the original *World of Warcraft*.

POLYMORPH

ONE OF THE GREAT JOYS OF BEING A MAGE in *World of Warcraft* is the ability to turn your opponent into a sheep, and the idea of showing that in the cinematic was floated during early brainstorming. "We actually put that in as a joke," confesses director Jeff Chamberlain. "There'd never been any real humor in our Warcraft cinematics, so we always kind of expected that it'd be cut. But it's an aspect of Warcraft that's always been there." Unfortunately, it turns out creating a CGI sheep is not as easy as you might think. To get the effect right, the cinematics team had to strike a balance between reality and fantasy—exaggerating and stylizing the sheep to fit the game aesthetic while keeping it easily recognizable as a sheep. "We went through many different hairstyles to find the optimal one," notes Samia.

When the time came to create the sheep for this shot, the team knew exactly whom to put on the task: Seth Thompson, a cinematic artist who grew up on a sheep farm.

ILLIDAN

"ILLIDAN WAS A LOT OF WORK. WE HADN'T DONE A CHARACTER LIKE HIM BEFORE. HE'S LEAPING UP, AND HE'S JUMPING THROUGH THE CLOUDS, AND HE HAS TO SORT OF FLOAT DOWN INTO VIEW. THAT WAS REALLY HARD TO GET RIGHT BECAUSE IT HAS TO LOOK NATURAL. THERE WAS NOWHERE TO GET IDEAS FOR THE MOVEMENTS—WE JUST HAD TO BE INVENTIVE."

—JAMES MCCOY, CINEMATIC ARTIST

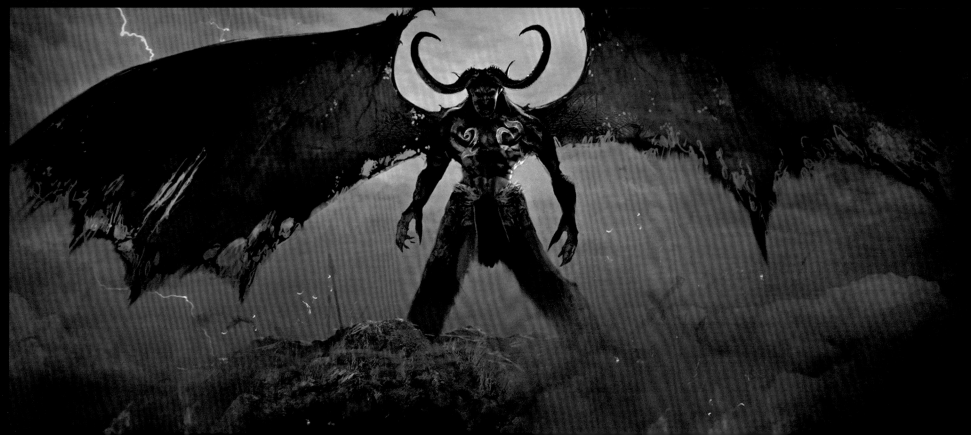

3
WRATH OF THE LICH KING

No sooner had the Horde and the Alliance returned from Outland than an old enemy stirred in the icy continent of Northrend. After years of ominous silence, the Lich King had emerged from his Frozen Throne, more powerful and confident in his purpose than ever before.

He announced his return with blood and terror. His undead Scourge swept over Azeroth, slaughtering hundreds of innocents and transforming them into mindless servants. And this was only the beginning. The Lich King's goal was nothing less than the complete domination of Azeroth.

To save Azeroth from the grip of death, the Horde and the Alliance would need to invade Northrend and confront the Lich King in the heart of his domain.

> "MY CHILD, I WATCHED WITH PRIDE
> AS YOU GREW INTO A WEAPON OF
> RIGHTEOUSNESS."
>
> —TERENAS MENETHIL

Brainstorming possible content for the *Wrath of the Lich King* cinematic, the team was naturally drawn toward the structure of the first two cinematics: a montage of action-packed, quick-cut shots that would give players a sense of the full scope of the expansion. Tossing out ideas, the team imagined the Lich King freezing ships full of Alliance and Horde troops as they make for the shores of Northrend. The cinematic might also show a day in the life of the tuskarr—storyboards depict the walrus-men dividing their time between fishing and fending off marauding undead Scourge. Other ideas involved undead versions of the fearsome half-giants called vrykul. But one idea in particular stuck: Arthas, the former prince of Lordaeron who fell to darkness and became the Lich King, emerges from his Frozen Throne to raise an undead dragon—the frost wyrm Sindragosa. "I remember thinking, man, that would be so cool, to just focus [on Arthas and the frost wyrm] and do nothing else," says director Jeff Chamberlain, "but it didn't seem like a possibility."

STORYBOARDS

'REMEMBER, OUR LINE HAS ALWAYS RULED WITH WISDOM AND STRENGTH. AND I KNOW YOU WILL SHOW RESTRAINT WHEN EXERCISING YOUR GREAT POWER."

—TERENAS MENETHIL

AFTER THE INITIAL BRAINSTORM, Chamberlain got together with storyboard artist Ben Dai to work out a few pitches to present to the game team. They decided to put the idea of Arthas raising a frost wyrm on the back burner, but they couldn't ignore it for long. "We knew that we should be focusing on the montage, but as we got to work, we both naturally gravitated towards this story. And we abandoned the montage idea." The pair produced a rough animatic made up of cut-together sections of the storyboards, backed by a narration from Arthas's father, and presented it to creative director Chris Metzen. Metzen was enthusiastic about the treatment, barring one big change—in those early storyboards, Arthas was shown riding the dragon, which wouldn't have fit his character.

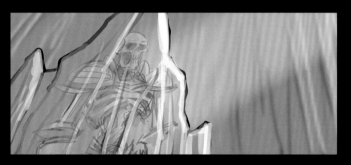

Early storyboards show Arthas freezing ships carrying invading Horde and Alliance forces and raising undead from the ice.

Explorations for a montage cinematic included tuskarr fishermen, ballista-wielding vrykul, and an explorer who scales a cliff only to find an undead army waiting.

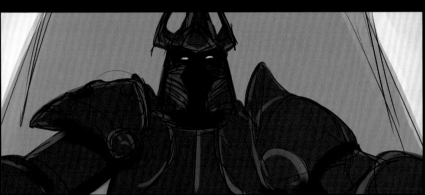

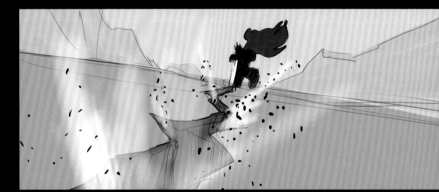

THIS PAGE AND OPPOSITE TOP LEFT
Frames from the cinematic's final storyboards.

OPPOSITE, TOP RIGHT AND BOTTOM
Detailed studies produced later in the process helped the team nail down compositions for the cinematic's thrilling climax.

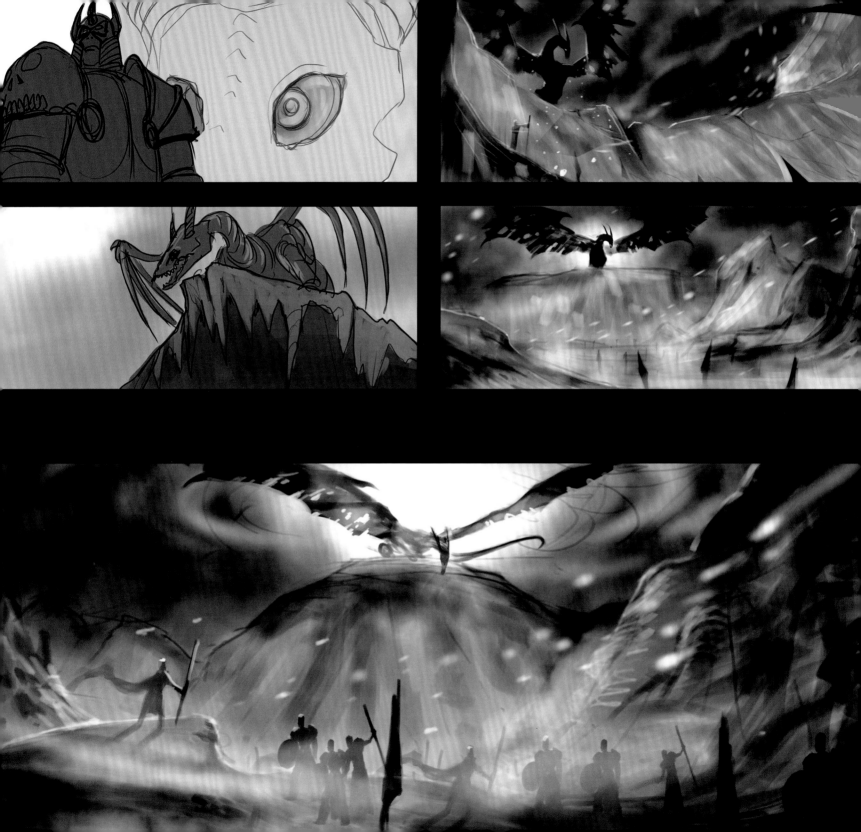

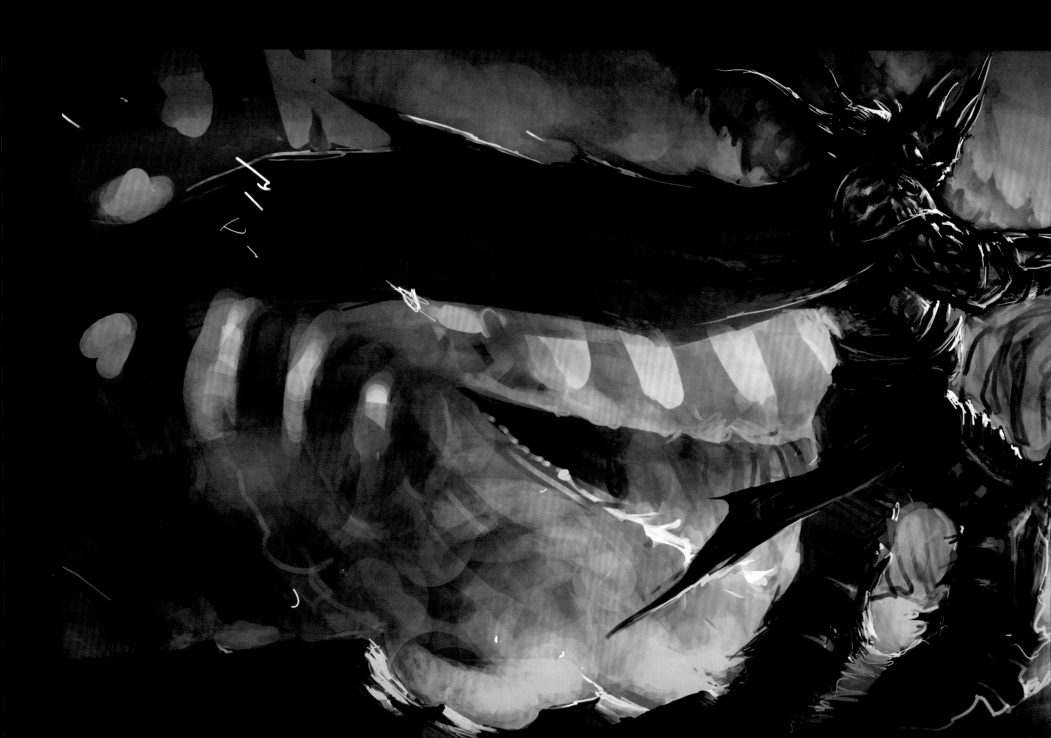

ARTHAS

"MY SON, THE DAY YOU WERE BORN THE VERY FORESTS OF LORDAERON WHISPERED THE NAME ARTHAS."

—TERENAS MENETHIL

THERE ARE FEW CHARACTERS IN *World of Warcraft* more steeped in lore than Arthas Menethil. One of the most beloved characters of the Warcraft franchise, Arthas is a tragic hero who has embarked on an epic saga of obsession and vengeance. In *Warcraft III*, Arthas spirals down a path of darkness, leading him to murder his father, King Terenas, and besiege his own kingdom. He is last seen ascending the Frozen Throne and donning the iconic helm that transforms him into the Lich King.

Concept art of Arthas with the undead frost wyrm Sindragosa.

OPPOSITE
Originally a passion project, this image was created by some of the cinematic team's artists in their downtime. It turned out so well that the marketing team used it.

THIS PAGE
Effect studies depict how Arthas's runeblade, Frostmourne, crackles with energy before he raises

THOUGH ARTHAS IS A CENTRAL CHARACTER in *Warcraft III*, the team had limited pieces of concept art for Arthas to draw from for the *Wrath of the Lich King* cinematic. "The few pieces we did have were a bit dated," explains director Jeff Chamberlain. In order to update Arthas's appearance, the team looked for the elements of his character that had remained constant over the years. Fan art proved especially insightful. "There's a buckle on Arthas's chest plate, for example. It's not super prominent, it's very small actually. But almost every single piece of fan art included it." By looking at the fan art, the team discovered what parts of Arthas have most resonated in players' minds. With an eye on the essential aspects of the character, the team was able to scale up Arthas's epic proportions and embellish his armor.

With Arthas's model cemented, the next step was to figure out how he should move. Because he is a character

with intent and focus, the animators aimed to keep his movements simple and subtle. His upright, ready stance signals he's prepared for battle at any moment, so the animators sought to break that upright posture as little as possible. There is also a ceremonial quality to Arthas's movements that helps convey the contrast between who he has become and who his father wanted him to be. "He was always going to be king, just not the way his father expected," notes cinematic artist James McCoy. This methodical animation style enhanced the storytelling, creating an air of mystery about what Arthas would do next.

Chamberlain wove in many references to Arthas's past life. After Arthas kneels to brush the snow from the ice where Sindragosa's bones lie, he briefly rubs the snow between his fingers—a callback to the way he catches a rose petal in a previous *Warcraft III* cinematic just prior to entering the chamber where he murders his father.

ABOVE
Arthas looks out over his army in the cinematic's final frames.

OPPOSITE
Concept art depicts the raising of Sindragosa from the ice.

FROSTMOURNE

THE DESIGN FOR FROSTMOURNE, ARTHAS'S infamous runeblade, changed very little from the *Warcraft III* cinematic to the *Wrath of the Lich King* cinematic. When Arthas draws the sword from its scabbard, a flare of light races across the edge of the metal. This small detail draws attention to the blade and helps it stand out from the cool, snowy environment and Arthas's metal armor.

"WHOMSOEVER TAKES UP THIS BLADE SHALL WIELD POWER ETERNAL. JUST AS THE BLADE RENDS FLESH, SO MUST POWER SCAR THE SPIRIT."

—INSCRIPTION NEAR FROSTMOURNE'S ORIGINAL RESTING PLACE

OPPOSITE
Artwork showcases Arthas wielding Frostmourne during the period prior to his transformation into the Lich King.

TOP
The Lich King's eyes flare to life before he rises from the Frozen Throne.

RIGHT
The final sketch of Frostmourne.

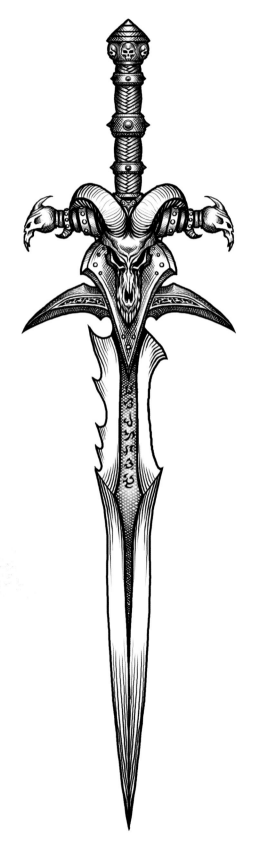

"BUT THE TRUEST VICTORY,
MY SON, IS STIRRING THE
HEARTS OF YOUR PEOPLE.
I TELL YOU THIS, FOR WHEN
MY DAYS HAVE COME TO AN
END, YOU SHALL BE KING."

—Terenas Menethil

Arthas prepares to raise Sindragosa
into his service.

SINDRAGOSA

LONG AGO, TRAGEDY STRUCK AZEROTH'S dragons. Neltharion, a noble defender of the world who would later become known as Deathwing, fell to corruption and brutally attacked his fellow dragons. Sindragosa was one of the victims. Severely wounded, she attempted to reach the safety of the Dragonblight, the ancestral home of her kind. She never made it, and her bones lay trapped atop Icecrown Glacier, frozen in time. At least until the Lich King raised her from the ice as his undead servant.

Early concepts for Sindragosa explored whether the dragon would have more of a bat-like design, with two legs and wings in place of arms or forelegs, or whether she'd have four powerful legs like other dragons in Warcraft. Settling on the latter, the team's challenge was how to convey the undead frost wyrm's scale and size. "It's hard to make skeletons look mighty, massive," explains Chamberlain. To magnify Sindragosa's presence, animators paid careful attention to poses and movement, conducting a number of sketch studies and deciding Sindragosa should move slowly, with powerful intention. Animators referenced the movements of birds and large reptiles like the Komodo dragon, as well as dinosaur movies. The cinematic also employs strategic camera angles to amplify the dragon: Shooting Sindragosa from ground level makes her movements feel even more massive and impactful.

LEFT
Sindragosa takes flight in a
color study.

OPPOSITE
Concept art envisions Arthas
visiting Sindragosa's remains,
locked in ice for millennia.

These sketches depict the fall of Sindragosa and the events leading up to her death. The black Dragon Aspect Neltharion created a powerful artifact called the Dragon Soul and convinced the other Aspects to empower the disk, promising that it would defeat the Burning Legion.

But at the time of their greatest need, Neltharion used the artifact to betray the other dragons.

Mortally wounded in the ensuing
battle and unable to reach the
Dragonblight, Sindragosa succumbed
to her wounds in Icecrown. It's here
that the Lich King finds her.

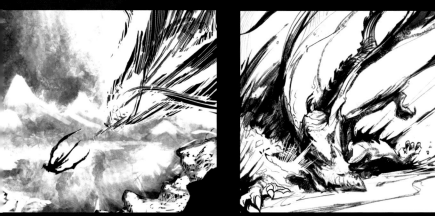

ABOVE
An early character study.

OPPOSITE
Concept art showing Sindragosa
soaring above Icecrown.

THE SCOURGE

THE LICH KING COMMANDS AN ARMY

of undead, the Scourge. After creating a number of
concepts, the team ultimately settled on two main "hero"
models that formed the basis for the rest of the army.
Small adjustments were made to armor and weaponry
to make each of the undead feel distinct.

UNDEAD
FOREGROUND

PAGES 68–69
Concept art for the rampaging Scourge
emphasized the decomposing skin and
musculature over their skeletal remains.

THESE PAGES
Final concept art for the heavily armed
undead Scourge.

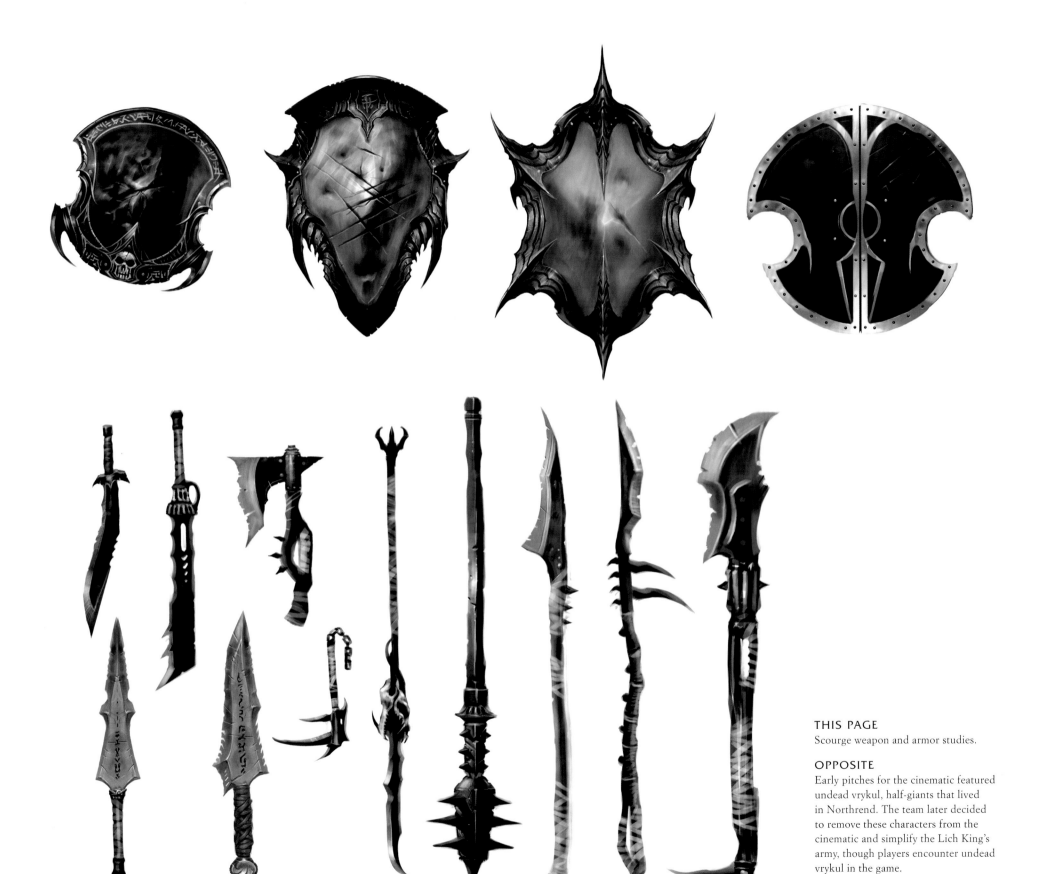

THIS PAGE
Scourge weapon and armor studies.

OPPOSITE
Early pitches for the cinematic featured undead vrykul, half-giants that lived in Northrend. The team later decided to remove these characters from the cinematic and simplify the Lich King's army, though players encounter undead vrykul in the game.

"SKELETONS ARE SUPPOSED TO
BE UNNATURAL—THEY'RE SHAKY
AND JITTERY. THAT MAKES THEM
A LOT OF FUN TO ANIMATE."
—James McCoy, Cinematic Artist

THESE PAGES
Early studies for the Scourge explore less armored models, undead females, and even undead tauren.

FOLLOWING PAGES
Jagged, icy peaks dominate the environment in Northrend concept art.

NORTHREND

WHILE THE *BURNING CRUSADE* EXPANSION
is marked by colorful environments, science fiction–like
with their neon greens and reds, the frozen continent of
Northrend presents harsh expanses of ice, snow, and
rock. To create Arthas's kingdom, the cinematics team
relied on matte paintings of the frozen environments,
which were then projected onto low-resolution mesh
geometry of the landscapes to give the scene depth.

The amount of ice needed made the cinematic one of
the team's most challenging productions ever. One of
the many challenges was making the ice crack and break
apart naturally—for example, when the Lich King rises
from his throne and when Sindragosa emerges from
the glacier. There was no simple solution. The team
projected paintings onto the geometry, employed special
effects, and adjusted lighting to create the final look.

But breaking the ice wasn't the only major undertaking.
"There's a fine line between ice and crystal," says
Steven Chen, a modeling artist on *Wrath of the Lich
King*. "How do you make it not look like a piece of
translucent glass?" Part of the solution was giving the
ice realistically complex coloring—an elegant mix of
turquoise, green, indigo, and other shades. Finding the
correct translucency and refractive quality was also key.
If these elements weren't perfected, Arthas would seem
like a miniature model sitting on a tiny glass throne.
So the team experimented with different methods of
lighting, modeling, and surfacing to make sure Arthas
and his throne were appropriately imposing and awe-
inspiring.

In a setting where everything has a cool, bluish palette, even tiny variations in color stand out. Lighting the environment was a challenge—lacking easy access to snow in Southern California, the team purchased eight gallons of fake snow to study how snow reflects light.

OPPOSITE
Concept art depicts Arthas shattering the ice
atop Icecrown Glacier and Sindragosa's return.

ABOVE
A final matte painting, which was projected on
low-resolution geometry to give the cinematic
depth. The team produced numerous color
studies to make sure every hue and tone works
in harmony throughout the cinematic.

IN-GAME CINEMATICS: THE WRATH GATE

'I WAS WONDERING IF YOU'D SHOW UP."

'I COULDN'T LET THE ALLIANCE HAVE ALL THE FUN TODAY."

—BOLVAR FORDRAGON AND DRANOSH SAURFANG

Led by Bolvar Fordragon, the Alliance begins the assault on the Wrath Gate by cutting through the undead Scourge until the barrier opens and a stream of vrykul arrive with a battle cry.

Just as the tide of battle seems poised to turn, Horde forces arrive to aid the Alliance. When Arthas emerges, Dranosh Saurfang rushes at him, only to be cut down by Frostmourne with a single stroke.

ANGRATHAR THE WRATH GATE WAS THE

massive armored entrance to Icecrown Citadel, domain of the Lich King. It was here that Horde and Alliance armies momentarily put aside their differences and stood united against their common enemy. But when the Lich King finally emerged from the Wrath Gate, things took an unforeseen turn. From a cliff above the battlefield, a small force of rebel Forsaken unleashed a toxic plague—an assault on the Lich King, but also a betrayal of the Horde and the Alliance.

"THE WRATH GATE" WAS *WORLD OF Warcraft*'s very first in-game cinematic, a groundbreaking moment that helped pave the way for the central role that cutscenes have come to command in the game. There's an emotional depth and complexity to the piece that, despite the simplicity of the underlying technology, has made "The Wrath Gate" one of the most beloved cinematics in all of *World of Warcraft*.

When director Terran Gregory read over the three-page script for "The Wrath Gate," written by creative director Chris Metzen and lead world designer Alex Afrasiabi, his jaw dropped. "I couldn't believe it, that they'd just put this entire cinematic in the video team's hands," says Gregory. "I spent a while grappling with the dissonance in my mind between excitement, and just, Do they realize what they just did?" To start, Gregory worked with storyboard artist David Durand, who drew over three hundred storyboards by hand, enough to cover an entire office wall from end to end. Some shots were cut—for example, the boards depict the moment when Alexstrasza, the red Dragon Aspect, sends out her followers to cleanse the blight. Over time, the boards were refined and camera angles determined.

Once the storyboards were approved, it was time to begin filming. Creating an in-game cinematic is quite different from creating a prerendered cinematic. Much of the technology

Under assault by a toxic plague, Bolvar Fordragon orders his troops to fall back. Unable to retreat in time, he falls to the ground, weakened. On the verge of death, he spots silhouettes in the distant sky.

After the Lich King's retreat, the red dragonflight soars above the Wrath Gate, incinerating the rebel Forsaken's catapults and cleansing the toxic plague with their enchanted flames.

Storyboards depict surviving Horde and Alliance forces looking on in awe at the dragons and a towering view of the Wrath Gate. These final frames were altered for the cinematic.

behind the "Wrath Gate" cinematic was the same as that used by the "machinima" community—the machine-cinema community of filmmakers who cut together original short films using gameplay footage. Animation often gets blocked out with simple commands available to any player in the game: "/sit," for example. Many things couldn't be AI driven. "If there was a crowd of people fighting in a combat cycle, that could be AI," explains Gregory. "But if there was a crowd of people running up stairs, or undead rising from the ground and assembling behind Arthas, then we needed actual players." To solve the problem, the team made use of digital extras, recruiting up to forty employees from Blizzard's Quality Assurance team to operate different fighters. "In hindsight, I think the most incredible part of 'The Wrath Gate' for me is that people still look back on it and see a cinematic," says Gregory. "Just behind the veneer was this elaborate system we were using to create that illusion."

4
CATACLYSM

The Lich King's reign had ended. As the Horde and the Alliance returned home to celebrate their victory, it seemed that the world would at last enjoy tranquility.

But it was not to be. Azeroth's elemental spirits heaved in unrest, setting off a slew of deadly natural disasters. Fear and uncertainty took hold in the Alliance and the Horde. What had become of their world? What was the cause of this elemental turmoil? Horde and Alliance leaders desperately searched for answers, but they were too late to make a difference.

Without warning, Azeroth reached its breaking point. Mountains crumbled. Fire engulfed the sky. Towering waves surged across the land and washed away entire towns. The deaths numbered in the thousands, but there were more to come.

The Cataclysm had begun.

> ## "PAIN. AGONY. MY HATRED BURNS THROUGH THE CAVERNOUS DEEPS."
> —DEATHWING

Released in 2010, *Cataclysm* shattered Azeroth. A chain of natural disasters ravaged the world—all the result of the terrible rage and elemental power unleashed by the expansion's main villain: Deathwing.

From the start, the cinematics team had two main goals for *Cataclysm*'s prerendered cinematic: to introduce the character of Deathwing and to showcase how the world was changing. The first two *World of Warcraft* cinematics had been montages, and *Wrath of the Lich King* was more story driven. But for *Cataclysm*, the team married these concepts into a visual travelogue of iconic locations, couched in a narrative revealing Deathwing's mindset as he prepares to wreak havoc on Azeroth.

DEATHWING

THE DRAGON ASPECT DEATHWING HAS
been known by many names over the course of Warcraft's
story. As Neltharion the Earth-Warder, he was charged
with the safekeeping of the earth and its lands—that is,
until he was driven mad and filled with rage. Deathwing
betrayed his fellow dragons, and over time he has even
disguised himself as a human to inflame tensions and
sow discord between the nations of Azeroth.

Though Deathwing was well established in Warcraft
lore, when work on the *Cataclysm* cinematic began, he'd
not yet been depicted in much detail. So the cinematics
team started with a short ideation period during which
artists were encouraged to explore different designs
and looks without restraint. Brainstorms around
volcanic, molten dragons abounded. But the team
quickly narrowed in on a few parameters. Some of the
concepts featured a two-legged Deathwing, but the
team wanted him to fit with the design conventions
of other *World of Warcraft* dragons, which have four
legs (such as the frost wyrm Sindragosa). With each
new piece, the artists sought to unlock Deathwing's
personality. "We knew he had to be nasty, aggressive,"
says director Marc Messenger.

OPPOSITE
An exploratory concept shows flames escaping from Deathwing's armor. Inspired by the regal look of a Brachiosaurus, the artist gave Deathwing a tall, elongated neck.

ABOVE
Deathwing posture studies.

OPPOSITE
Final concept art for Deathwing.

ABOVE
A rough sketch of Deathwing's reinforced jaw.

RIGHT
As concepts progressed, the dragon was slowly given more bulk and heft, with a larger body proportionate to his wings.

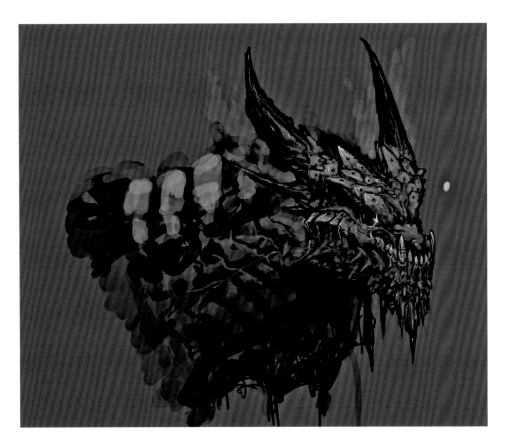

Various treatments for Deathwing's face helped the team explore the dragon's attitude and character. Each concept carries its own sense of menace, and some help convey the dragon's insanity.

ONE PIECE IN PARTICULAR REPRESENTED A turning point—a concept by artist Glenn Rane. While aspects of Deathwing's final design are already apparent in the piece, what it really represented for the team was an attitude. Here's Deathwing in all his glory—mighty, battle-scarred, and menacing. "It gave us a compass heading to steer by," notes Messenger.

OPPOSITE, TOP RIGHT, AND RIGHT
Artwork explores Deathwing's ever-growing metal jaw.

ABOVE LEFT
Glenn Rane's concept.

Various treatments for the pattern arising from Deathwing's chest and armor. In the above early concept, Deathwing is shown with several layers of armor that have built up over time—yet the molten fury inside still shines through.

DEATHWING'S ARMOR

WITH GLENN RANE'S CONCEPT IN HAND, THERE WAS still a lot of work to do. The most drastic refinement was in Deathwing's armor. The molten fury running through Deathwing's veins was so powerful that it disfigured him and threatened to destroy him completely. More than once in the Warcraft saga, he has had armor bolted over his wounds to keep his body from tearing apart. For this latest incarnation, the team explored a metal jaw for the dragon. As soon as the first iteration hit, the team knew they were on to something. And then the jaw kept getting bigger. "We just kept pushing it," laughs Messenger. "We kept saying, What if it was *bigger*?" Deathwing's elementium-plated jaw became an iconic aspect of his silhouette and a quick way to differentiate him from any other dragon.

But the work of Deathwing's followers, the Twilight's Hammer cult, to reinforce his body didn't stop with the addition of his jaw. "You can see, on his chest, that it's all just splitting apart in the middle because his rage cannot be contained," explains Messenger. Deathwing's molten, glowing chest became another of the character's essential visual cues. The team treated the glowing red pattern on the dragon's chest almost like a rune, or a symbol. It's definitive to the character—unmistakably Deathwing. In addition to the neck and spine plates established in the lore, the cinematics team created a range of metal staples or stitches to hold him together. In one shot, the camera pulls back along Deathwing's torso as massive battering rams nail armor to his body. Originally, the nails were hard to see in the dim surroundings, so the team decided the nails should glow and spark at the moment the battering ram hits them. These effects also convey just how much force it takes to armor Deathwing, and how painful the process is.

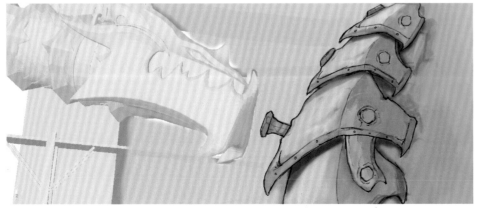

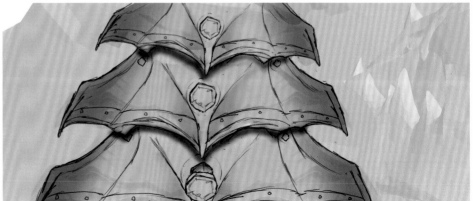

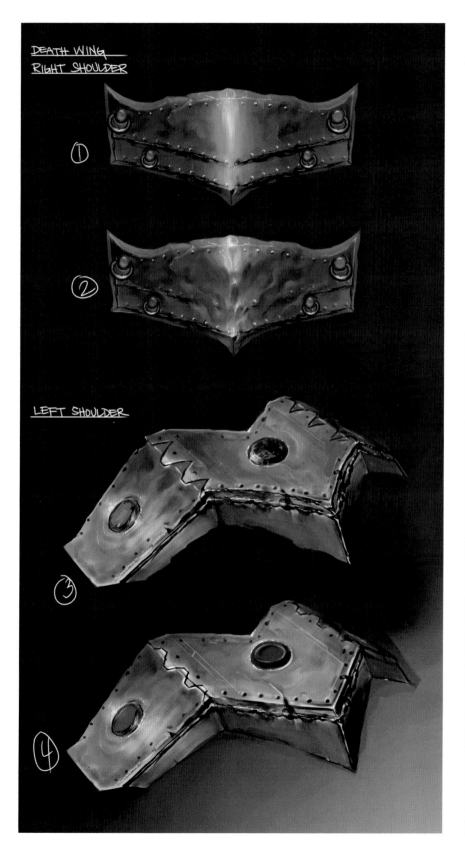

DEATH WING
RIGHT SHOULDER

① ②

LEFT SHOULDER

③ ④

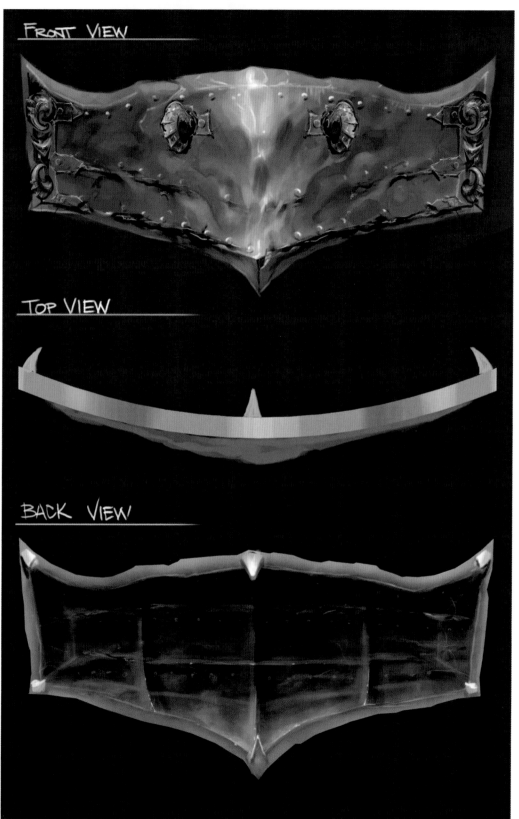

FRONT VIEW

TOP VIEW

BACK VIEW

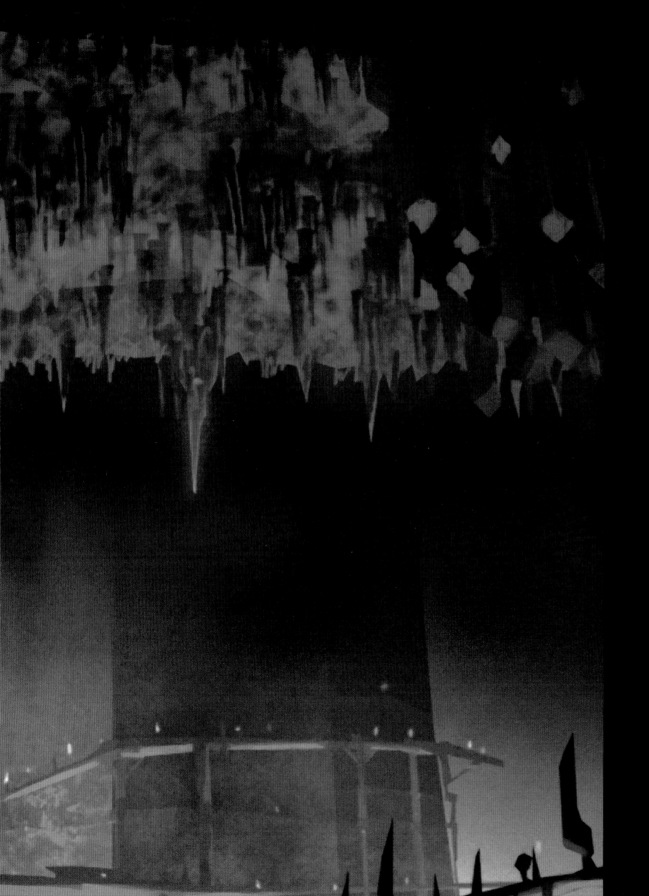

DEEPHOLM IS AN ANCIENT AND

mysterious place. Long ago, powerful beings called the keepers created this domain as a prison for earth elementals. But that didn't keep Deathwing from finding his way inside and using it as his lair.

Though players would eventually journey to Deepholm in the game, the zone was still in the early stages of development when work kicked off on the cinematic. A number of concepts were explored—the team was keenly aware that the appearance of Deathwing's lair would profoundly affect the character and how players see him. For example, when the keepers first created Deepholm, it was beautiful, with majestic chambers defined by columns and crystalline structures. So one of the main debates among the team was how much of that beauty would remain in Deathwing's corner of Deepholm. Eventually, it was decided that the area was deeply scarred by Deathwing's presence—shrouded in darkness, fire, and lava, revealing only a hint of what it once was.

WHEN NEAR COLUMNS
CAN HAVE ADDITIONAL
SUPPORTS ATTACHED TO
ROCKS

CAULDRONS OF
MOLTEN ELEMENTIUM

MORE SPIKES!
EVERY 5TH ONE
IS A LARGE
SPIKE

PLATFORMS WHERE
COLUMNS ARE CAN
BE MORE DECORATIVE
AND FATTER

EVERYTHING IS JUST
SUMMONED, SO ALL
MADE OF ELEMENTIUM

CAPITAL - WINGED,
SPIKEY MOTIFS ON
SIDES (×4)

LIGHTS TO HELP
SCALE

BATTERING RAM LOOK

SUMMONED ITEMS COULD HAVE
PLATED, LAYED LOOK. SHOULD LOOK
LIKE THE SAME HAMMERED MATERIAL
DEATHWING'S ARMOR IS MADE OF

MIX & MATCH PARTS

COLUMNS SUPPORT CATWALKS
CATWALKS SPAN THE REST

The Twilight's Hammer cult has surrounded Deathwing with cranes and scaffolding as they reinforce him with elementium plates.

Deepholm's columns are carved from crystal but blackened by soot and surrounded by lava—a testament to how the dragon has scarred this place.

To convey the dragon's size and scale, it was decided that the viewer would only see parts of him for the first half of the cinematic, as he stirs in his lair.

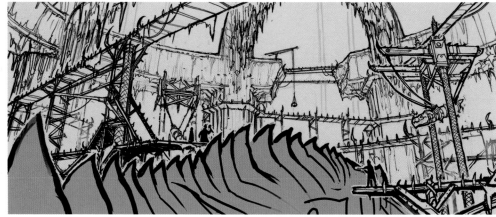

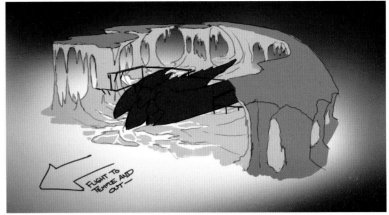

LEFT
An early concept for the Twilight's Hammer battering rams. It was decided that even the winged sail at the top of the structures would be made of elementium, since other materials would likely catch fire.

TOP AND ABOVE
Overviews for the Deepholm set show the dragon nestled tightly against the confines of the space.

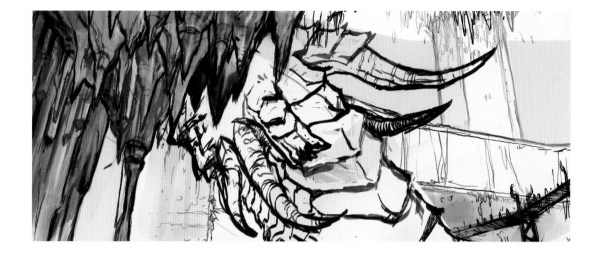

Designs for the cult's battering rams featured elaborate dragonlike motifs as a testament to the cult's worship of Deathwing.

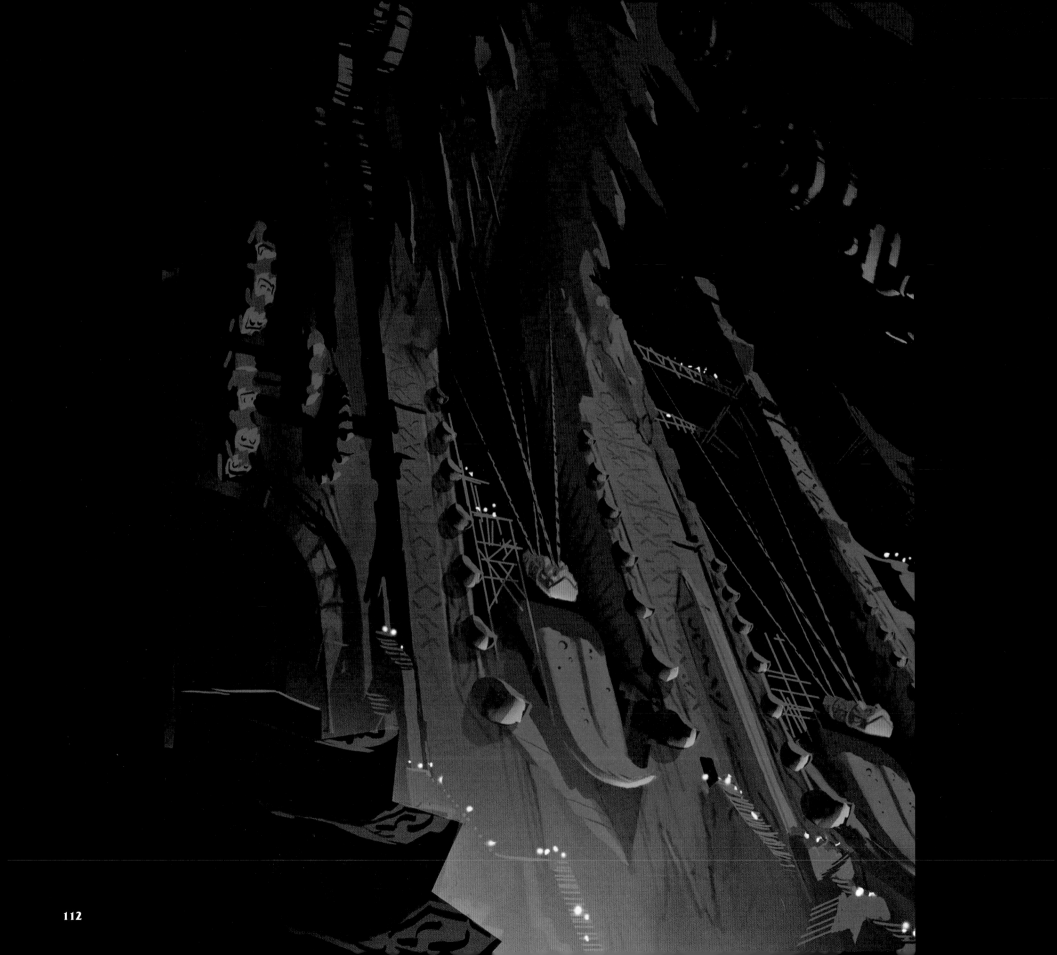

Reinforcing Deathwing's armor required an elaborate operation. The filmmakers wanted to convey the complexity of the undertaking with a myriad of tools and structures and then show the dragon's careless destruction of them as he makes his exit from Deepholm. The crumbling structures help echo the chaos rippling on Azeroth's surface.

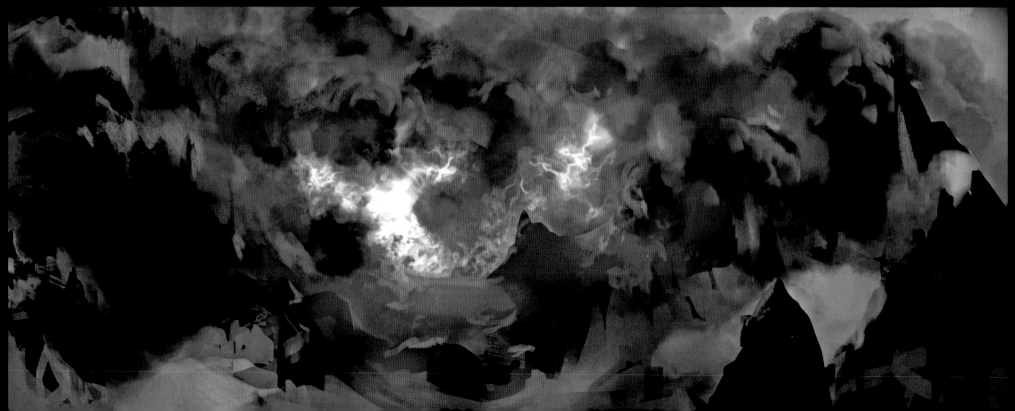

DESTROYING ENVIRONMENTS

"THE WORLD HEAVES WITH MY TORMENT. ITS WRETCHED KINGDOMS QUAKE BENEATH MY RAGE."

—DEATHWING

THE GAME TEAM USED *CATACLYSM* TO thoroughly reimagine the world of Azeroth, bringing drastic changes to Kalimdor and the Eastern Kingdoms. So the cinematics team had plenty of options of environments to work with. In deciding where to set their movie, the team thought a lot about what they were calling the Statue of Liberty syndrome. "What would it mean if the Statue of Liberty got destroyed before your eyes? What kind of devastating emotional impact would that have on the average American? On anybody?" asks Messenger. The team tried to connect with this idea, searching for iconic places within Azeroth, landmarks or cherished symbols of culture, that players would see and think, "I've been there. That place means something to me."

A variety of locations were storyboarded—lava boils out from Ironforge, a firestorm ravages through Thunder Bluff, the Stonetalon Mountains are blown to pieces—but not all of them made the final cinematic. The team evaluated their many options based on level of fan recognition and the strength of the image itself, while seeking balance between Alliance and Horde locations. The final selection includes Darkshore, Loch Modan, Thousand Needles, Orgrimmar, and Stormwind. Deathwing's return would change them all forever.

THE BARRENS

Located outside the Horde seat of power in Orgrimmar, the Barrens is a setting intimately familiar to many as a Horde zone that innumerable players leveled through in their earliest days. It's a setting many find nostalgic to this day, making for a ripe opportunity to begin to show Deathwing's destruction.

Taking iconic in-game settings and increasing their fidelity for a cinematic involves a flow of collaboration between the cinematics and game teams. Both teams must contribute to decisions on how to enhance a scene while retaining the images players know well.

"It's always a challenge to translate in-game environments into our prerendered cinematics," says Messenger. "Very early on, the cinematics team started going for broke in terms of really wanting to make it a hyperreal environment, where you know that everything is high fantasy, but it still all feels real, it feels believable." Accomplishing this means using lighting, textures, and composition to their full potential. A sunset, for example, will feature extra color tones and cloud formations, presenting an idealized version of reality.

The team created concepts for various orcish huts, but only the tower was used in the final cinematic.

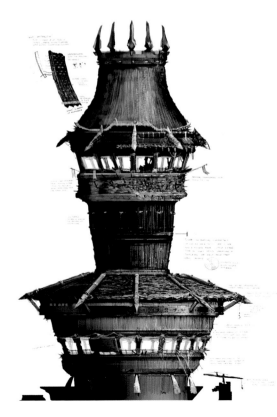

An important part of the concept process is the commentary artists make about their intent and inspiration for a piece, as well as any idiosyncrasies in the design that might be overlooked by other artists.

Creating the goblin zeppelin required a healthy mix of attention to detail so that it would be believable that the vehicle could fly, as well as plenty of cut corners and rickety aspects of design, which players expect from goblin engineering.

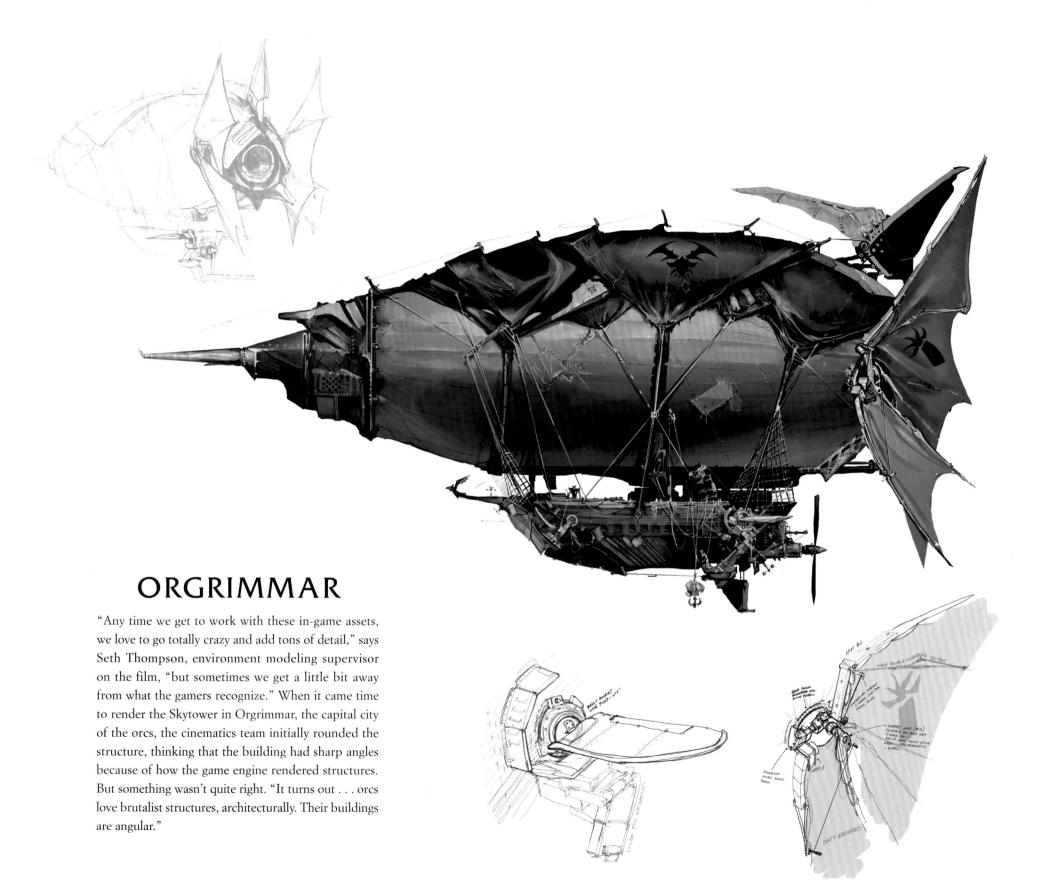

ORGRIMMAR

"Any time we get to work with these in-game assets, we love to go totally crazy and add tons of detail," says Seth Thompson, environment modeling supervisor on the film, "but sometimes we get a little bit away from what the gamers recognize." When it came time to render the Skytower in Orgrimmar, the capital city of the orcs, the cinematics team initially rounded the structure, thinking that the building had sharp angles because of how the game engine rendered structures. But something wasn't quite right. "It turns out . . . orcs love brutalist structures, architecturally. Their buildings are angular."

DARKSHORE

The structures around Darkshore were built by the night elves, so the process of bringing them into higher fidelity was deeply informed by the culture of that race. "Originally, in our first series of concepts, we had made it feel a bit old, as if it had been built ages past," says producer Phillip Hillenbrand. But it wasn't long before the team realized something was off. Night elf architecture is well-kept and without any obvious flaws—this aspect of their culture was lost as the cinematics team tried to punch up the level of detail on the buildings by aging them. The team shifted their attention to rendering the buildings as perfectly as possible—only the individual planks on the pier structure, with algae barnacles clinging to their undersides, were spared this treatment.

The team looked to the game wherever possible in building each set, down to the shapes and variance of the trees surrounding Darkshore.

Concept art for the pier in Darkshore, before and after its brush with Deathwing. The pier's silhouette was simplified as work on the cinematic progressed, with the ramshackle supports and railings removed to better reflect the precision of night elf architecture.

LOCH MODAN

Historically, the lake of Loch Modan was held in place by the enormous Stonewrought Dam, an architectural wonder featuring large dwarf faces carved into its side. Deathwing's return shook the dam to its foundations, crumbling the familiar dwarf faces and unleashing a deluge of water.

While the cinematics team originally wanted to show more of the dam, the physics of destroying the dam and having water burst through its cracks was a challenge. The team hadn't created that kind of fluid simulation before, and there was no example from the real world that they could use for how the carvings of these giant dwarf faces would crack and fall away. Getting it right meant experimenting with all disciplines—from animation, modeling, lighting, and texturing—until it felt believable.

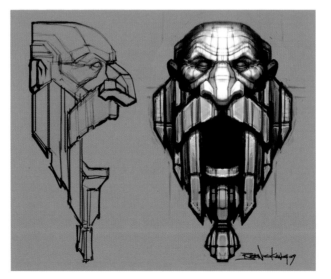
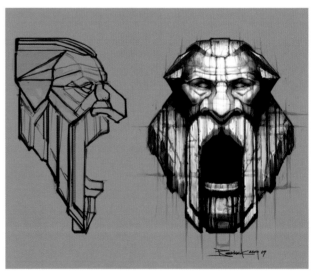

Though the carved faces of the dam are indistinguishable from one another in the game, the cinematics team created unique looks for each, as if they were modeled off dwarven heroes.

STORMWIND

The human city of Stormwind is the seat of power for the Alliance, making its gates and the surrounding forest one of the most iconic locations in all of *World of Warcraft*. Apart from being a perfect place to show Deathwing's rampage, it also serves as a thematic bookend—a way to visually convey that a dark shadow has fallen over the world. "When we first see Azeroth up top, the sun is out, it's glorious. We showcase the beauty of the world," says Marc Messenger. "But as we progress through the scene, the sun gets lower in the sky, the world gets dimmer. So by the time Deathwing shows up at Stormwind, the sky has gone dark. The fire has spread in around the gates. And it's giving an echo of that hellish environment that we started with."

THOUSAND NEEDLES

The *Cataclysm* cinematic is essentially a disaster movie, and as such, the enormity and preponderance of effects was a major challenge. Mountains of water, curtains of fire, spewing lava, sparks—every shot featured major effects. One of the most challenging effects was Thousand Needles. In the cinematic, the arid, dry canyon floods, and many of the towering mesas familiar to fans come crashing down. "It was initially a very different-looking shot," notes digital effects supervisor Mike Kelleher. "The wave was going to tower above us and then come crashing down on our camera position." But the sheer level of detail required to render the wave from top to bottom was impossible. Pressed for answers, the team actually found a better shot by bringing the wave much closer to the camera. The feeling is visceral: You're definitely not going to get out in time.

These concepts show just how far out the wave that crashes through Thousand Needles begins, in addition to exploring various shapes for the towering stone structures.

BOOTY BAY

IN-GAME CINEMATICS: GOBLINS AND WORGEN

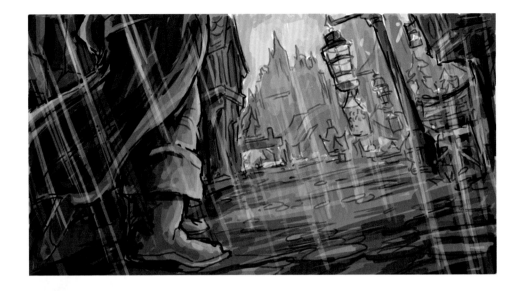

"IS THERE EVEN A SHRED OF HUMANITY LEFT WITHIN YOU? PERHAPS. WE WILL FIND OUT, SOON ENOUGH."

—LORD GODFREY, WORGEN INTRODUCTION

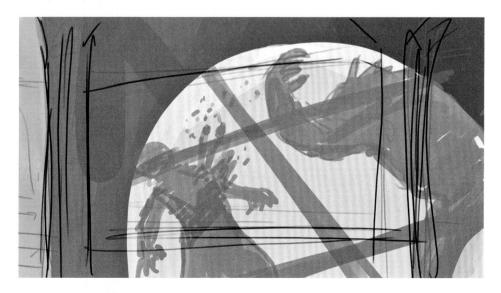

ORIGINALLY, THE CINEMATICS TEAM HAD planned to showcase *Cataclysm*'s two new playable races in the expansion—the goblins and the worgen. Storyboards were created showing the goblins evacuating from a volcanic eruption on their island, as well as a sequence involving a skirmish between Alliance and Horde that is suddenly interrupted by the arrival of worgen. "We usually cast a pretty wide net, story-wise, but then we go back and refine," says Messenger. In the end, the sequences were cut from the prerendered cinematic in favor of creating dedicated cinematics for each race in-game.

IN THE STORYBOARDS FOR THE WORGEN introduction, the in-game cinematics team drew from familiar horror elements—a caged monster, a dreary landscape, dark, bold silhouettes. The protagonist of the cinematic is Lord Godfrey, a nobleman of Gilneas. The model for the cinematic is a heady mix of repurposed parts: The character required a heavy cloak for his stark silhouette—so the team borrowed Arthas's cloak geometry. For his glasses, the team took a pair off the Ozzy Osbourne character created for the 2008 *World of Warcraft* commercial featuring the rock star. And Lord Godfrey's face was adapted from the model of the human paladin Tirion Fordring.

Of course, repurposing can only take the animation so far. For the worgen cage, the cinematics team had to go into the in-game environment of the internal build of the

game and pry off boards, nails, and surrounding fences to hew the ramshackle cage together. Interestingly, the improvisation results in a design that looks exactly as you might imagine a *World of Warcraft* character in that harsh environment would have created.

While *World of Warcraft*'s prerendered cinematics have aimed for hyperreal depictions of the game, the philosophy behind the in-game cinematics is that they should stay true to the visuals of the game itself. The aim is to present a seamless transition, with a bit of refinement to help immerse players in the story. "What we want is just to add a bit of shadow, add more lights, a reflection of the worgen's eyes in Godfrey's glasses," says director Terran Gregory. "All that adds up."

5
MISTS OF PANDARIA

The Cataclysm did more than reshape the lands of Azeroth—it left deep political divides between the Horde and the Alliance. After Deathwing met his demise, the factions did not forge a peace; they turned their wrath against each other. Tensions between the Horde and the Alliance took on a new ferocity, sparking a battle for control of Azeroth that spilled into a new land . . .

Shrouded in an enchanted mist for ten thousand years, the ancient realm of Pandaria had long remained unspoiled by war. A place of lush forests and cloud-ringed mountains, it was the home of the pandaren, a wise race fond of harmony—and strong ales.

But the arrival of the Horde and the Alliance shatters the tranquility of Pandaria and threatens to awaken old evils that have been locked beneath the earth for years.

"FOR MY KIND, THE TRUE QUESTION IS: WHAT IS WORTH FIGHTING FOR?"
—CHEN STORMSTOUT

Illidan. The Lich King. Deathwing. The first three prerendered cinematics of *World of Warcraft*'s expansion sets focused on some new villain or global crisis that the Alliance and the Horde have to face. With *Mists of Pandaria*, however, the villain is something altogether different—war itself. Pandaria was a place hidden from the world for thousands of years, a place of balance and hope. That is until the old Horde and Alliance conflict arrives, with all of its hate, violence, and factional conflict.

Telling the story of this new land and its people required a lighter touch and a more intimate setting than the sprawling montages and apocalyptic disaster sequences of earlier cinematics. Early on in the production process, the story arrived almost fully formed—the Horde and Alliance interlopers wash up on the shores of Pandaria and bring their red vs. blue conflict with them. But in this strange, seemingly deserted place, they're surprised to find a thriving civilization.

"WHY DO WE FIGHT? TO PROTECT HOME AND FAMILY. TO PRESERVE BALANCE AND BRING HARMONY."

—Chen Stormstout

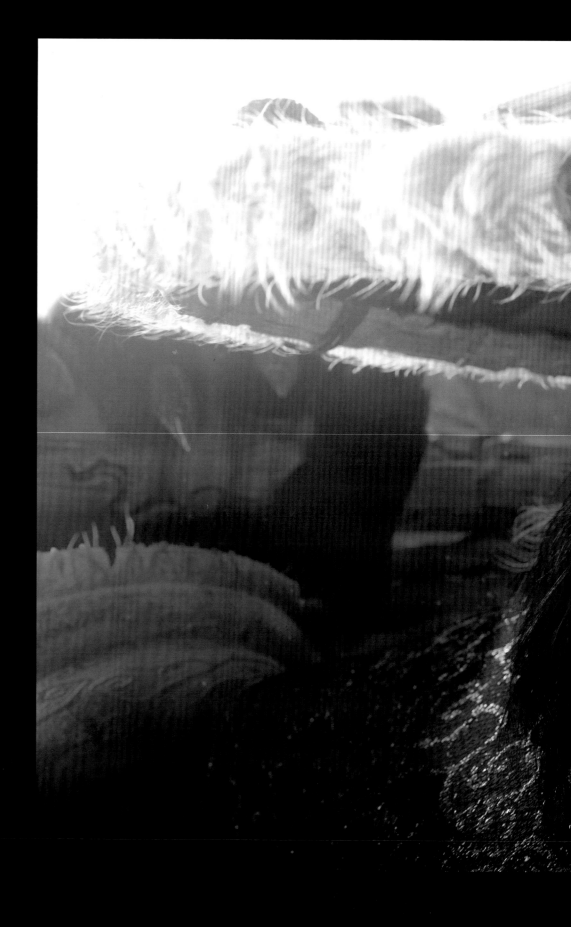

CONCEPT EXPLORATION

THE PANDAREN HAD EVOLVED AS A culture apart from the rest of Azeroth. The cinematic needed to communicate just how different this new race is. "This was a chance to be a little bit lighter, a little more playful. So we just embraced that opportunity from all disciplines, not just in the storytelling but in the design, characters, and animation," says director Marc Messenger.

Early concepts for the *Mists of Pandaria* cinematic's three characters: the pandaren, the human, and the orc.

MISTS OF PANDARIA'S PRERENDERED cinematic marked the first departure from the hyperreal aesthetic that had been developed for the previous *World of Warcraft* cinematics. "We had been accustomed to taking the in-game models and then just detailing them like crazy," says art director Chris Thunig. With *Mists* came an opportunity to reflect and be more intentional about the art style of the cinematic. "We tried to pull back on the realism a bit and go a little bit more stylized with the characters. The captain, the orc—they're pushed a little bit in anatomical and facial structure. They're more fun and whimsical." By making hyperdetailed characters based on stylized geometry, a new Blizzard style started to emerge. "The geometry says, 'I am not a real human being.' But the detail says that I am organic, I am alive," says Messenger.

The change in art style called for an extended ideation period in which the production allowed all the artists in the department to just *paint*. Artists heard a basic pitch of what the cinematic was to be and then had free rein to draw orcs, humans, pandaren, and environments— throwing out designs for anything they thought might be interesting. There were more pieces of concept art for *Mists* than for any previous cinematic.

Equally important as finding the right attitude and look for a certain character was making sure the three characters fit together thematically. Many artists applied a certain visual style or motif to all three characters in order to see what worked.

SHELL EARRING

SHARK TOOTH

THIS PAGE
In concepts for the pandaren character, the team skewed toward depicting him as older and grizzled. They began to think of him as a veteran.

OPPOSITE
One of the few concepts of a young pandaren.

Artists experimented with a variety of armor and wardrobe options for the pandaren, trying everything from regal attire and ornate armor to traditional martial arts uniforms and shabbier clothing.

In keeping with the cinematic's nautical theme, artists looked for ways to explore the orc's connection to the sea, with concepts often giving him an eye patch or adorning him in shell or shark-tooth jewelry.

Artists explored everything from size and hairstyle to weapons and armor throughout the ideation period. While most pieces weren't used for the final cinematic, they helped narrow down which visual cues were working and often inspired work on other projects.

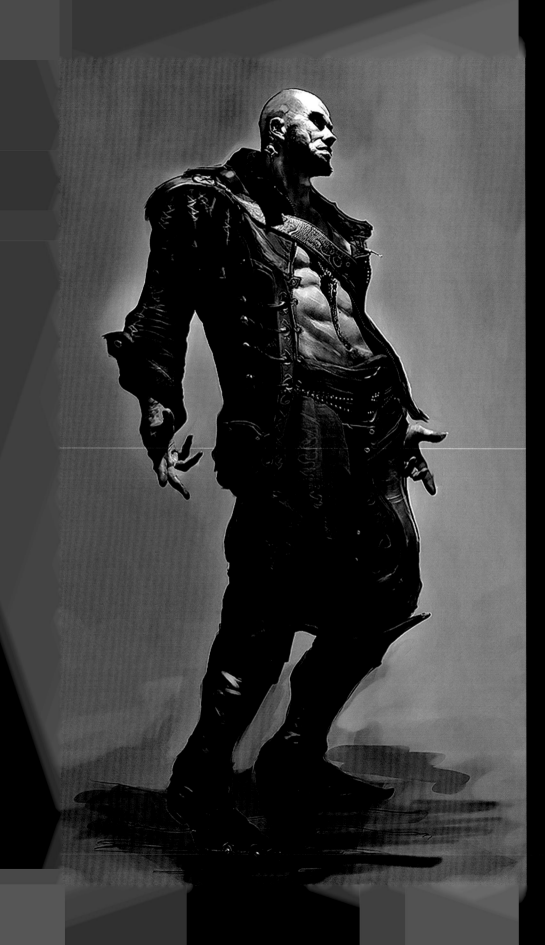

In reviewing concepts from the ideation period, the team sought to highlight which elements were working and refine them. The open jacket featured on several of these pieces was a quick favorite, as were the naval epaulets (*above*), which fit with Warcraft's stylized, big shoulders.

· CHEWING AND SPITTING OUT TABACCO.

· FLIPPING AROUND SHORTSWORD ONCE IN AWHILE.

· PICKING TOOTH W/ SWORD

· DRAGGING SWORD IN DIRT + THROWING DIRT AT OPPONENT.

The team started to think of the human character as a man a bit past his prime who has spent much of his life at sea, so it made sense that he wouldn't be clean-shaven. Artists explored various facial hairstyles in concept art and 3D models.

THE HUMAN CAPTAIN

AS DESIGNS FOR THE HUMAN CHARACTER accumulated, his backstory and personality took shape. The team saw him as a ship's captain—a gritty survivor. He was someone who wouldn't be afraid to fight dirty, especially to protect the Alliance. The human was also an imposing figure, the kind of burly soldier that just might be able to stand toe to toe with an orc grunt. The team latched on to certain elements from the early concepts and refined them for the final design: the size of the captain's jaw, his mutton chops, and his blue captain's jacket, which was an organic way to show his ties to the Alliance.

OPPOSITE
Almost-final concept art for the ship's captain. For the cinematic, the character's gloves were removed, and his undershirt was torn further to reveal more of his burly chest.

LEFT AND TOP LEFT
Frames from the color script.

ABOVE
A digital paintover of a 3D render, used to fine-tune the look of the captain.

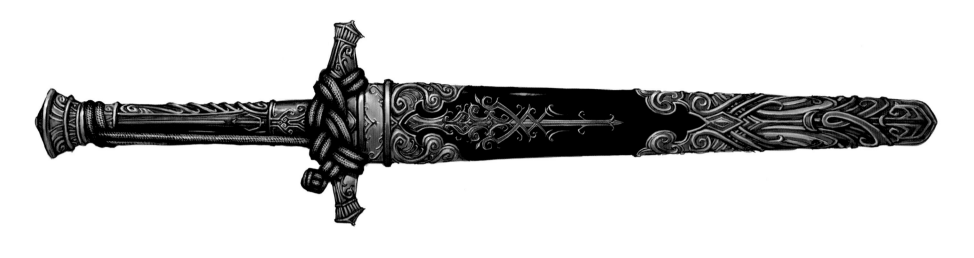

THIS PAGE
Concept art for the ship captain's scabbard, broken sword, and improvised spear.

OPPOSITE
Sketches map out a range of potential facial expressions for use in the cinematic.

CRUNCH!!
NOT THE
"MONKEY STEALS
THE PEACH"
TECHNIQUE !!

THE ORC GRUNT

THE ORC THAT APPEARS IN THE CINEMATIC is an orc grunt in a classic way. He's adorned in a single, spiked shoulder pad—the most basic orc outfit, familiar since the days of early Warcraft. While early versions of the orc show him armored, it was decided he'd shed much of it as he desperately swam to shore after the shipwreck. And the character would be easier to animate if he wasn't bogged down in armor. As with the human, the orc's personality came out as the artists iterated. The shipwreck was personal to him. A lot of his Horde comrades died on that ship, and he's furious—he would do anything for them. He's incredibly strong, but in his anger, he doesn't think before he acts. He forges into the unknown terrain, heedless of any dangers that might be waiting.

OPPOSITE
Concept art showing the orc's many battle scars—his old wounds hint at a long history of warfare.

While the decision to keep the orc light on armor made him easier to animate in the sense that his armor wouldn't restrict his movements, it made it challenging to show so many muscle groups flexing and firing.

THE CINEMATIC ART OF **WORLD OF WARCRAFT**

OPPOSITE
Concept art shows how the orc was refined in stages to feature a more stylized facial structure, less armor, and just the right number of wounds from the shipwreck.

ABOVE
A paintover of a 3D sculpt of the orc, done without armor to give artists a clear look at his anatomy.

RIGHT
Sketches map out potential facial expressions.

THE PANDAREN

THE CINEMATIC WAS TO FEATURE THREE original characters—a human, an orc, and a pandaren. During concept exploration, several designs for the pandaren were tossed about. Some of them were young, but many were older, more wizened pandaren with variations of regal armor.

In Marc Messenger's storyboards, which came even earlier, the director had tended to draw him a bit like Chen Stormstout—the pandaren character from *Warcraft III*—since that was the only reference he had at that point. When Messenger presented the storyboards to the game team, *Warcraft III* art director Sam Didier was invited along. "We had Sam come check it out because Chen is sort of his baby boy," says Messenger. "And he said after the meeting to me, 'So that was Chen, right?' and I said, 'Oh, actually, we're going to create an original character.' He said to me, 'Oh, I thought that was Chen. How come it can't be Chen? And I thought to myself . . . well, how come it can't?"

OPPOSITE
Concept art for the pandaren includes a musical instrument strapped to the character's back.

THIS PAGE
Artists tried to adhere to a cohesive visual style for the pandaren elements in the cinematic, making sure that even props and materials that have little screen time feature details appropriate to the character's culture.

THE CINEMATIC ART OF **WORLD OF WARCRAFT**

OPPOSITE
A frame from the color script.

THIS PAGE
Artists also explored armored
versions of the pandaren.

BELOW
Concept art for Chen Stormstout.
One of the main differences between
this version and the final was the
character's eyes, which were changed
from green to gold.

OPPOSITE
Sketches map out various movements
and poses for Chen in the cinematic,
conveying a sense of speed and grace
despite his size.

ANIMATION

WITH *MISTS*, ANIMATORS HAD FUN TRYING to apply the more traditional, stylized animation style to Warcraft's characters. "It's a little Chuck Jones," explains Messenger, referring to the legendary animator known for his work on Looney Tunes and Merrie Melodies shorts. The cinematic has a staccato rhythm with frequent pauses. One key moment is the shot where Chen grabs the incense burner out of the air, slams it down, and then realizes it needs just a slight adjustment—which he makes with his staff. And then the twig moves in his mouth. "We kept looking at that shot in animation and thinking, we want this to be funny, why isn't it? And we realized that we were still injecting so much naturalism into it," says Messenger, referring to the many subtly animated elements, from breathing to uneven movements, that the team had been accustomed to applying for heightened realism. The more the animators stripped away all these details and started to treat Chen essentially as a statue who moves just enough to fix the incense burner, the funnier the shot became.

The human ship's captain makes his way warily up the steps in frames from the color script.

FACIAL MAPS

THE PACING OF THE ANIMATION ALLOWS the viewer to constantly refer back to the character's faces—when the orc grunt takes a hit to the face, the movie pauses just enough for viewers to appreciate his expression. Similarly, when the human captain cuts off part of Chen's straw hat, the pause lets viewers take in Chen's glowing eye. The whimsical art style that had been honed during concept exploration allowed

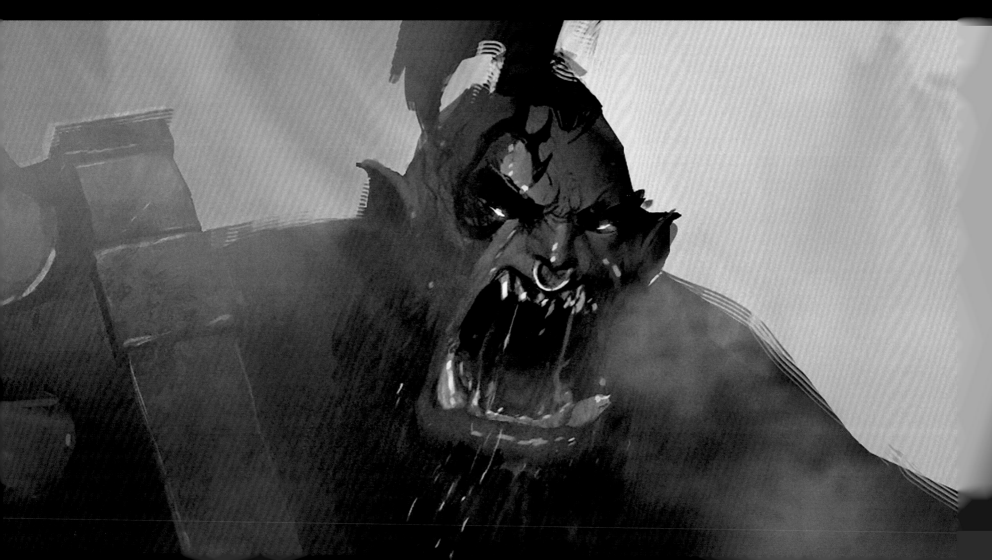

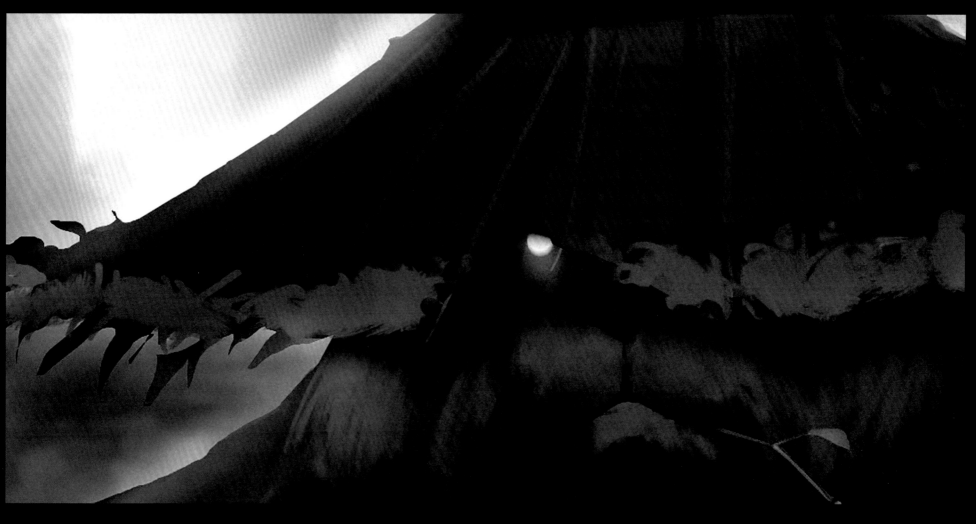

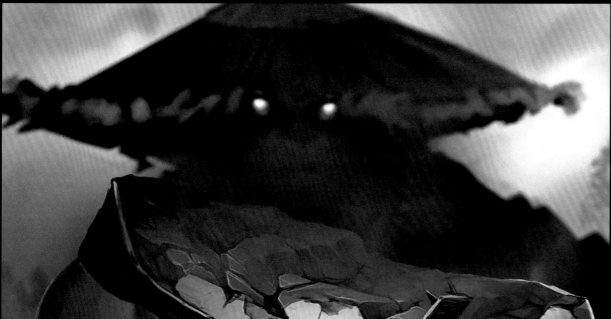

for these believable facial expressions. "We knew that if we stylized the characters and their faces, we'd be able to avoid the uncanny valley," says Thunig, referencing the phenomenon where realistic depictions of humans in 3D animation tend to feel strange and off-putting compared to more stylized versions. "They'd automatically become a little bit more forgiving when we'd have the characters emote."

The production mapped out all the emotional beats of the story and drew detailed facial expressions for each moment. The resulting model sheet indicates whether or not the character will work in all situations. While previous cinematics used a sculptural approach to facial expressions, the sheer number of close-ups in *Mists* required new technology that could map out and mimic the muscles in the face.

FIGHT CHOREOGRAPHY

THERE'S A LOT OF MELEE COMBAT AND martial arts in the *Mists* cinematic, but the team didn't employ a choreographer. "We initially thought we were going to need a fight choreographer to come in, but the search for the right person dragged on long enough that we had shot a lot of stuff ourselves. And we were having a lot of fun," explains Messenger. While not necessarily looking to be completely realistic, the production did want to be truthful. By shooting video reference of team members acting out fighting moves on one another, the team mined little gems and naturalisms that they transferred to the animated characters. One moment of video reference stands out: Cinematic modeler Jeramiah Johnson had an affinity for acting out the orc's moves, and the team needed some reference for the scene in which the orc charges at the human and winds up careening into a statue that comes crumbling down. "We set up a pad and had Jeramiah act out the moment. And we asked him to run into the pad as hard as he could. He really gave it his all, so much so that he broke one of the walls in the office," says Messenger.

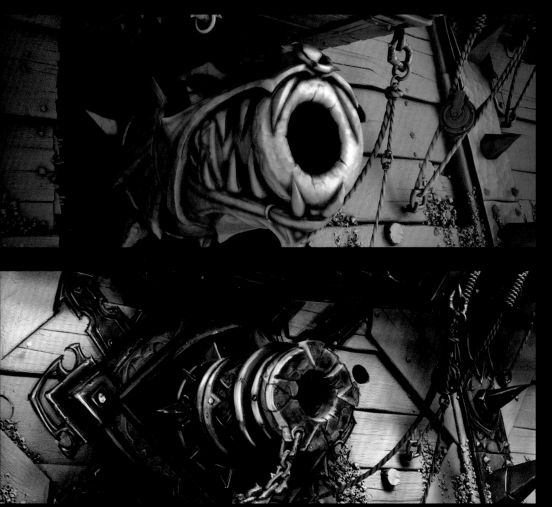

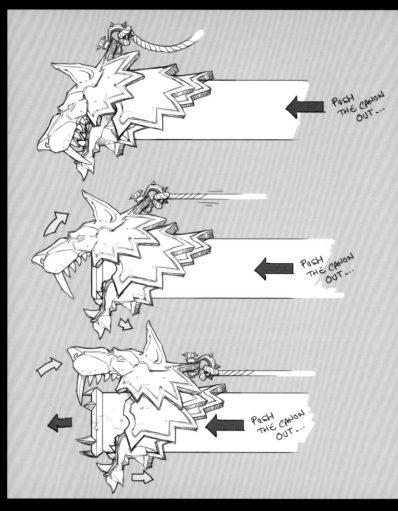

PUSH THE CANON OUT...

PUSH THE CANON OUT...

PUSH THE CANON OUT...

A naval theme hadn't been explored in a Warcraft cinematic since *Warcraft II: Tides of Darkness*, so there was little to base the Horde ship on. Special attention was paid to detailing the ship's cannons, which are given a close-up at the start of the cinematic. While concept art envisions the cannons emerging from a wolf's mouth, the team ultimately settled on a simplified final design (*opposite center left*).

BELOW
Final concept art for the Horde ship.

WE BUILT THE ALLIANCE SHIP ORIGINALLY FOR *CATACLYSM*.
IT WAS ONLY MEANT TO HOLD UP IN A DISTANT SHOT. BUT THEN
WHEN WE WENT TO DO *MISTS OF PANDARIA* WE SAID, 'WELL,
WE HAVE THIS BOAT. LET'S GO AHEAD AND PUT IT IN THE SHOT AND
SEE HOW IT FEELS.' IMMEDIATELY WE FELT LIKE IT WASN'T NEARLY
DETAILED ENOUGH, SO WE GOT TO WORK FLESHING IT OUT."

—MARC MESSENGER, DIRECTOR

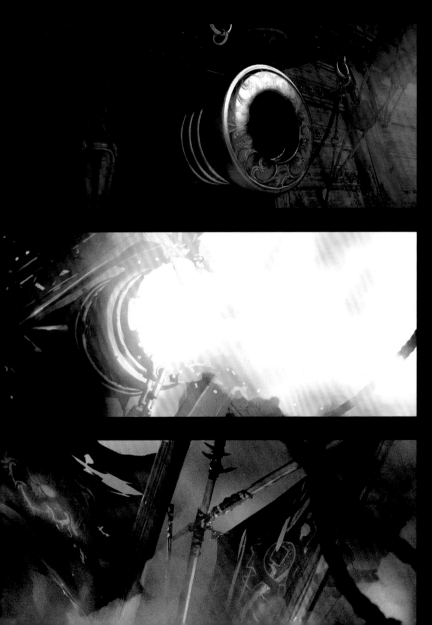

THE SHORE

FOGGY AND MOODY, DIM GREENS dominate the shoreline and the environments as the human and the orc ascend into a strange, unknown land. The color palette and environmental effects were key elements of storytelling in the cinematic. The fog and use of shadows keep this new location a mystery and play up the tension and fear among the shipwrecked characters.

Occasionally, visual effects artists find ways to insert Easter eggs from other Blizzard games into *World of Warcraft* cinematics. Instead of normal insects, the bugs for this shot are actually zerg from *StarCraft II*—tiny mutalisks, overseers, overlords, and corruptors placed in the cinematic by an artist who had just finished working on a piece for *StarCraft II: Heart of the Swarm*.

Concept art for the mysterious shore, which is shrouded in fog.

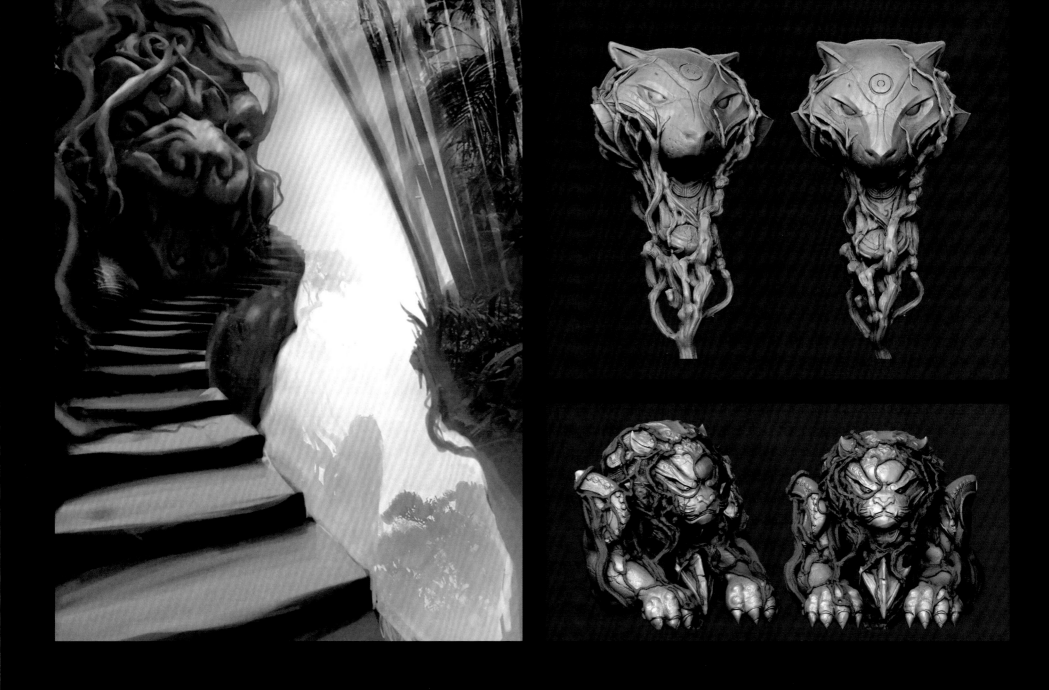

The statues and totems that line the
path from the shore to the Shrine of
Fellowship are covered in twisting

THE SHRINE OF FELLOWSHIP

WHEN THE FOG CLEARS AROUND CHEN'S staff toward the end of the cinematic, a sweeping vista is revealed. Based off some screenshots of an early build of the in-game location, the cinematics team worked to increase the detail and fidelity of the space so that when players visit the Shrine of Fellowship in the game and climb up to the plateau, they'll realize they're visiting the same place that Chen battled the orc grunt and human ship captain that washed up on Pandaria's shores.

OPPOSITE
The Shrine of Fellowship, as seen in the cinematic.

BELOW
An early sketch exploring the design of the area where the human, orc, and pandaren characters fight.

BOTTOM
A frame from the color script.

An essential part of the visual
storytelling of the cinematic is the
move from the misty shore to
the shrine, where light permeates
the scene once Chen pushes away the
fog by slamming down his staff.
These pieces of concept art from
the ideation period were used later
to help guide the lighting process.

LEFT
In crafting the Shrine of Fellowship and the surrounding environment, the team sought to make clusters of intense detail in vast areas of calm, with elements such as a lone cherry blossom tree on a cliffside. The decision helped give the area a feeling of serenity but also wonder.

OPPOSITE
A key concept art piece, which helped guide the visuals and stylization of the cinematic.

BOTTOM
A frame from the color script.

Texturing and determining materials is an integral part of the cinematic process. For *Mists of Pandaria*, the artists used idealized versions of materials like metal or wood, exaggerating them to fit with the film's saturated colors and stylized character models.

OPPOSITE
The incense burner used by the orc as a weapon, from concept to 3D model. Artists carefully applied moss and cracks to the item to help enrich the design.

ADD ORANGE TINT TO
GOLD PAINT IN AREAS
WITHOUT MOSS TO
MAKE IT FEEL A LITTLE
LESS FLAT AND MAKE
GOLD PAINT FLAKY

IN GENERAL DON'T
HESITATE TO ADD
CRACKS AND WEAR
TO AGE ASSET (BUT
DON'T DESTROY
READ)

ADD A BIT MORE
CONTRAST BETWEEN
MATERIALS

ADD TOP DOWN MOSS
PASS AND DARKEN
CREASES BY ADDING
GRIME TO MAKE
SHAPES/CARVINGS
MORE READABLE

SELECTIVELY
ADD DETAIL FOR
COMPOSITION
(E.G. BIRD SHIT, LICHEN,
STREAKING),
CHECK IN CAMERA
FOR HERO ANGLES

CHOOSE A NUMBER
OF GRAIN LINES THAT
WILL STAND OUT AND
SUBDUE UNIMPORTANT
DETAIL BY OVER-
PAINTING WITH 50%
OPAQUE BRUSH

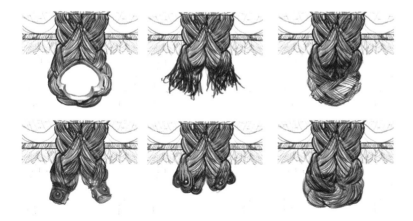

Once the fog is pushed away, a vast backdrop of mountains comes into view. To envision the environment, artists referenced rock formations such as the South China Karst.

THE BURDENS OF SHAOHAO

> "IF HE WAS TO SAVE HIS LAND AND HIS PEOPLE, HE WOULD BE CALLED TO DO SOMETHING GREAT. . . . HE WOULD SACRIFICE ALL THAT HE WAS."
>
> —*THE BURDENS OF SHAOHAO*

EARLY ON IN THE DEVELOPMENT OF *Mists of Pandaria*, the expansion's lead quest designer, Dave Kosak, gave a presentation to the game team telling the story of the last emperor of Pandaria—Emperor Shaohao. Dressed as Lorewalker Cho, the great historian of the pandaren people, and wielding a large red staff, Kosak told the story of the emperor and how Pandaria came to be surrounded by the mists: *Young Shaohao was born to be emperor and wanted for nothing. The wealth of the great pandaren empire was his to command. Consulting the Great Waterspeaker, Shaohao expected to hear of his long life and prosperous realm—but instead, Shaohao learned of terrors that awaited the world. To save Pandaria from the Sundering, Shaohao would have to unburden himself—from doubt, despair, fear, anger . . .*

RIGHT
The opening painting of the series' prelude.

OPPOSITE TOP
The ancient empire of Pandaria on the day of Shaohao's coronation.

OPPOSITE BOTTOM
Shaohao chases after the Monkey King, who has been carried away with a gust of wind.

LEFT
One of the first paintings of Emperor Shaohao, which helped guide the visual development of the cinematic.

OPPOSITE
The jinyu waterspeaker, whose vision of the Sundering set the events of *The Burdens of Shaohao* in motion.

CAPTIVATED BY THIS STORY, A SMALL TEAM began work on what would become *The Burdens of Shaohao*. The six-part series marked Blizzard's first foray into a style of animated storytelling now referred to as "motion story." *Burdens of Shaohao* was conceived as a kind of storybook, with a voice-over narration played over a series of about thirty multilayered paintings per episode. The paintings could be pulled apart and edited to create limited animation and special effects. In fact, the entire series was planned to take place over a series of scrolls, with the camera panning down the length of the scroll onto different scenes. But this was deemed too restrictive a format as Shaohao's story evolved.

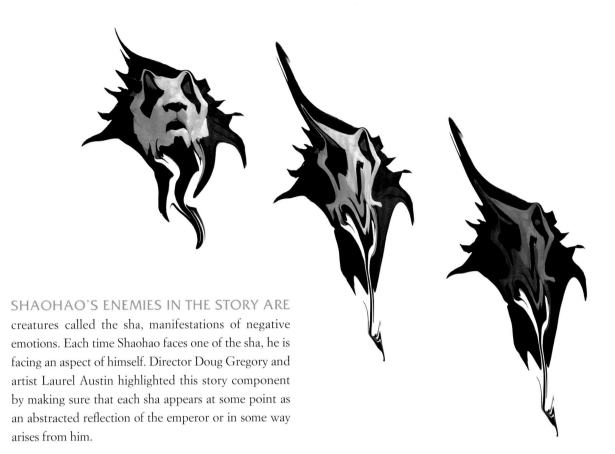

SHAOHAO'S ENEMIES IN THE STORY ARE creatures called the sha, manifestations of negative emotions. Each time Shaohao faces one of the sha, he is facing an aspect of himself. Director Doug Gregory and artist Laurel Austin highlighted this story component by making sure that each sha appears at some point as an abstracted reflection of the emperor or in some way arises from him.

OPPOSITE
Concepts of the sha arising
from Emperor Shaohao from
"Part 4: Anger."

THIS PAGE
Paintings from "Prelude: The
Vision," "Part 1: Doubt," and
"Part 2: Despair."

Coming to the land of the mantid, Shaohao is overcome with fear. Under the advice of the mighty Black Ox, the emperor refuses to turn away.

ABOVE AND TOP RIGHT
Rough color concepts used to block out the scene for final painting.

6
WARLORDS OF DRAENOR

During the war in Pandaria, the Horde's unity was tested. Its brash leader, Garrosh Hellscream, had become a warmongering tyrant. His dream of reforging the Horde into a more brutal, orcish ideal caused the faction to splinter from within. The growing unrest triggered a full-scale rebellion, leading to the overthrow of Garrosh and his loyalists.

But death was not Garrosh's fate. For his crimes, he was put on trial. The Horde and the Alliance both hoped that this would bring closure to a dark chapter in Azeroth's history, but before Garrosh's verdict was read, he escaped.

Not just from his holding cell, but from the present. He traveled to a past version of Draenor, the ancestral home of the orcish race and the birthplace of the Horde.

> "DRINK, HELLSCREAM. CLAIM YOUR DESTINY. YOU WILL ALL BE CONQUERORS."
>
> —GUL'DAN

Warlords of Draenor introduced players to a world already steeped in lore, a place that existed before the orcs became corrupted with demon blood. A place that would be shattered into the realm known as Outland. Once the cinematics team knew that Garrosh would journey to a past version of Draenor, they had many questions to answer. How would they envision the lands of this lost world? How would they depict the orcs? And, perhaps the greatest question of all, *when* would Garrosh arrive?

STORYBOARDS

AN EARLY PITCH FOR THE *WARLORDS OF Draenor* cinematic had Garrosh traveling back to the Siege of Shattrath, to the moment when the orcish Horde sacked the draenei city with a combination of fel magic and war machines. But relatively quickly, the team settled on a different idea: a council of clans.

In these early storyboards, all the orc leaders of old have assembled to elect their first warchief. And the warlock Gul'dan is present, his skin green from the fel blood flowing through him. Gul'dan's aim is to sway the orcs to accept the demon blood as he did, promising that it will transform them into incredibly powerful warriors. The council is forced to make a decision: Would they side with the demon lords and drink their blood, or would they go their own way? Into the fray, a mysterious cloaked figure would arise—Garrosh Hellscream, an orc from the future.

The moment when the orcs decide to drink the demon blood is a powerful one. It's a moment that goes back to the very origins of Warcraft—in the original timeline, the demon blood corrupts the Horde, kills their world, and drives the orcs to invade Azeroth. But the council of clans idea didn't quite resonate with the team.

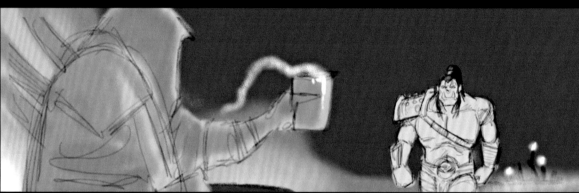

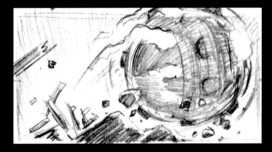

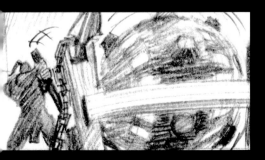

ULTIMATELY, THE TEAM WENT BACK TO THE stories—the lore that had built up over the years. "It was staring right at us, saying, 'When you're ready, I'm right here,'" says director Marc Messenger. "The scene where Gul'dan offers the blood of Mannoroth to Grommash Hellscream, we realized, was the perfect venue for telling our story. It was a point that everybody was familiar with, and a point where you could change history."

In the original telling, Mannoroth isn't actually present when the orcs drink Gul'dan's poison. Or rather, Mannoroth isn't seen. Perhaps, the team thought, Mannoroth is present but cloaked in magic. And so Garrosh's plan starts to come together: Not only will the orcs not drink the blood, but they'll pour out the offering and see if they can't lure the pit lord out from the shadows. With the idea solidified, the team knew what characters, environments, and weapons they would have to create.

THE ORCS OF DRAENOR

IN TRAVELING TO DRAENOR, GARROSH Hellscream encounters his father, Grommash—the legendary chieftain of the Warsong clan and the first in line to drink the demon blood. When he's last seen in *Warcraft III*, Grommash Hellscream is green, with glowing red eyes—symptoms of the demonic power flowing through his veins. But the *Warlords of Draenor* cinematic takes us back prior to the blood pact, when the orcs were uncorrupted. The team sought to depict these orcs as more primal in nature—they have more leathers, furs, and bones incorporated into their armor.

In addition to comprehensively reimagining the orcs, the cinematic had to visually distinguish the main characters so they'd be easy to recognize in a dimly lit space. But there also had to be hints of the lineage between Grommash and his son Garrosh.

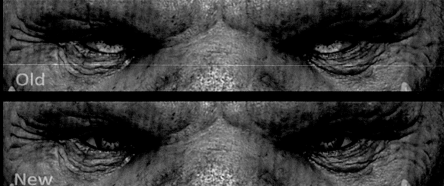

From his first inclusion in *World of Warcraft*, Garrosh Hellscream's eyes have been integral to his character. "Through his many iterations, he's always had that amber glow in his eyes," explains Terran Gregory. "He's a predator in the dark at all times." Finding the right hue for Grommash's eyes helped identify him as Garrosh's father.

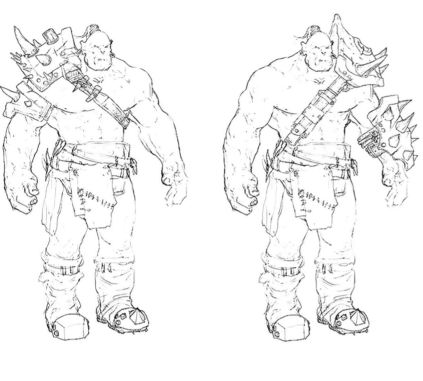

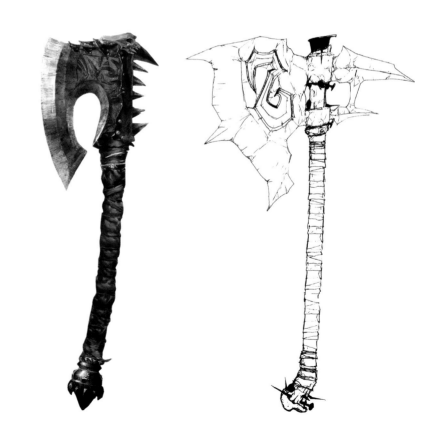

ABOVE AND TOP RIGHT
Armor studies.

RIGHT
3D model of Grommash's legendary axe, Gorehowl.

FAR RIGHT
Sketch for an axe wielded by orcs in the crowd.

Blizzard Cinematics Character Modeling
8/7/13

OPPOSITE
Textured 3D model of Grommash.

THIS PAGE
Renders of Grommash, chieftain
of the Warsong clan.

A RETURN TO HYPERREALISM

IN *MISTS OF PANDARIA*, THE CINEMATIC aesthetic is lighthearted and whimsical. But the mood of *Warlords* is dark, dramatic. It tells of a pivotal moment in Warcraft's history, set on an unforgiving and bloody world. So the team aimed to push its traditional hyperreal aesthetic further than ever and create orcs that feel in every way believable. "It's not easy to make skin look like skin and sweat look like sweat," explains Messenger.

In crafting the detailed orcs, the team focused on capturing the subtlety of the character performances. "We knew we had orcs with big jaws and big tusks, but they needed to work close up, speaking," explains art director Chris Thunig. By digging out small features in the face and making sure they all fire together in symphony, animators make it possible to know what Grommash is thinking before he utters a word. Water shaders were placed under the skin of the models so that at different points during the cinematic, beads of sweat would form on the characters and refract against their skin. Garrosh and the other orcs were also given peach fuzz in the form of thousands of tiny hairs across their bodies.

Similar attention was paid to Grommash's musculature. Almost two hundred maps were created dedicated to firing off muscles in different parts of his body, from biceps to triceps down into his neck tendons.

These 3D models of Grommash were refined to make the orc feel as believable as possible.

GUL'DAN

GUL'DAN WAS AN ORC WHO ALLIED himself with the Burning Legion for personal gain. His demonic masters tutored him in the ways of fel magic, and he became the first orc warlock. But his new strength came at a price, which the cinematic team incorporated into his design. Gul'dan's entire body shows what he has sacrificed in his quest for power, from his twisted posture to the signs of decay on his upper lip. For all of the main characters in the cinematic, the team used lighting, texturing, and effects to draw attention to their iconic traits so that it was always clear, even from a distance or in shadowy lighting, who they were. For Gul'dan, his red eyes and the curved spikes on his back set him apart.

"AND WHAT, GUL'DAN, MUST WE GIVE IN RETURN?"

—GROMMASH HELLSCREAM

LEFT
When Grommash asks what price the orcs will pay for this new power, Gul'dan pulls back his hood and replies, "Everything." Iterations of Gul'dan's eyes helped explore how bright they would glow in this moment.

OPPOSITE
Textured 3D model of Gul'dan.

GUL'DAN IS A GUY WHO WILL GO TO ANY LENGTH, AND SACRIFICE ANYONE, TO GAIN POWER. IT'S NOT ABOUT HATING OTHER PEOPLE. IT'S NOT ABOUT SOME CIVILIZATION OR SOME OTHER PERSON THAT HAS DONE HIM WRONG. IT'S ALL JUST STEPPING STONES TO ASCEND OUT OF THIS DOLDRUM EXISTENCE."

—CHRIS METZEN, SENIOR VICE PRESIDENT OF STORY
AND FRANCHISE DEVELOPMENT

OPPOSITE
Detailed concept art for Gul'dan shows the warlock without his robes and many of his accoutrements.

THIS PAGE

MANNOROTH

"YOU WOULD REJECT THIS GIFT? AND
DID YOU BRING THESE MONGRELS HERE
JUST TO WATCH YOU DIE?"

—MANNOROTH

FIRST SEEN IN *WARCRAFT III*, MANNOROTH is a demon pit lord originally responsible for corrupting the orcs of Draenor. Since he hadn't been seen in a cinematic in over ten years, the team wanted to take the opportunity to conduct a major upgrade. There were some immediate challenges, however. "Here was a character that doesn't have any lips, doesn't have any eyelids," says art director Chris Thunig, "so he doesn't give us that much to work with." The team produced a variety of concepts to try to apply the latest technology to the model, but in the end, they found themselves adhering more and more to the original. "With everything we did to him, he started to not look like Mannoroth anymore," explains Thunig. It was important that the latest model would ring true to fans familiar with *Warcraft III*. "There's some sentimentalities that come with the character, and it's a fine line to walk." The final model increased Mannoroth's fidelity, especially in his musculature, but he remained closer to the *Warcraft III* cinematic than any other character in the *Warlords of Draenor* introduction.

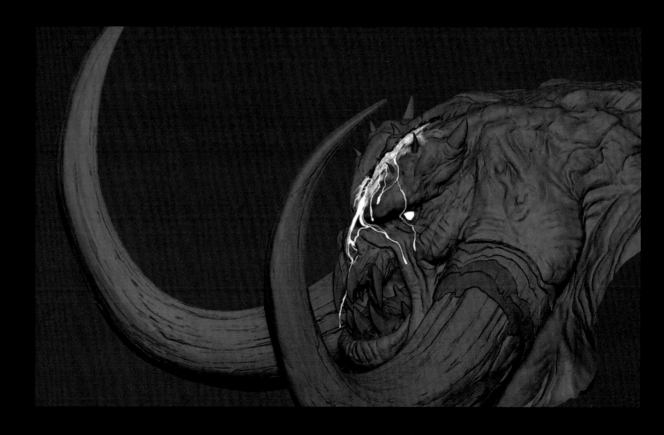

OPPOSITE
Renders of Mannoroth.

ABOVE
Concept art explores how blood would spill from Mannoroth's forehead after the pit lord receives the killing blow from Grommash.

The team explored myriad ways of updating Mannoroth's look, from adding bulk to heightening the more grotesque aspects of his facial structure, before settling on more subtle refinements of the *Warcraft III* model.

OPPOSITE BOTTOM LEFT AND OPPOSITE CENTER
The effects team produced numerous concepts for the magic Mannoroth unleashes from his weapon, experimenting with how smoky or fiery the blast of energy should be.

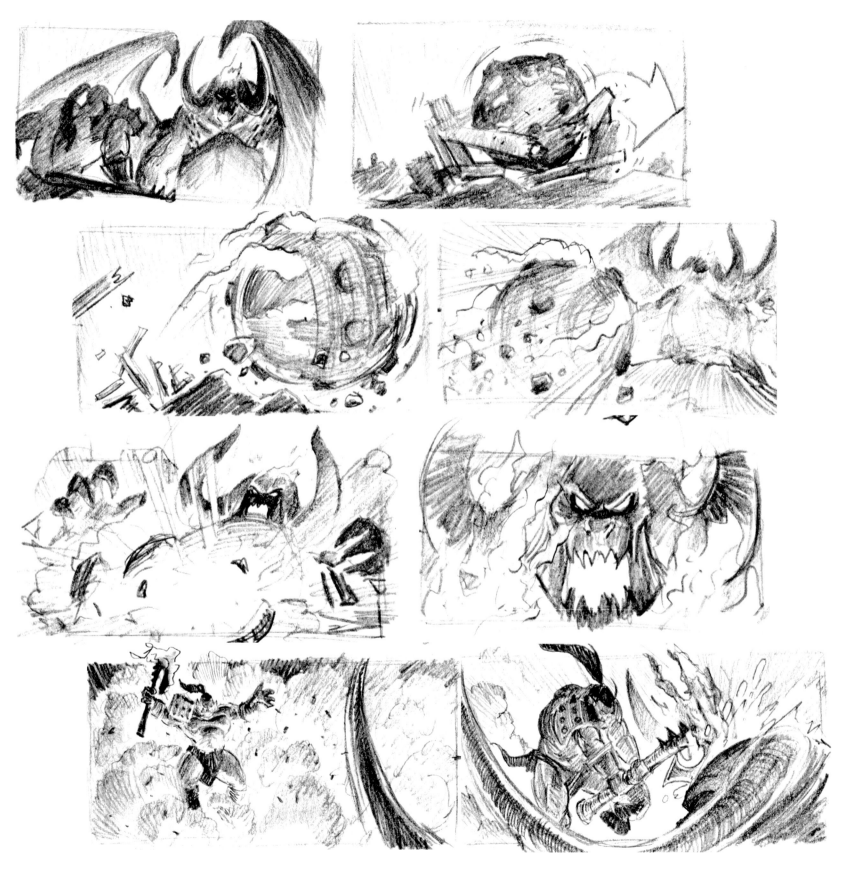

THE IRON STAR

WHAT COULD GARROSH OFFER THE ORC chieftains to reject the blood of Mannoroth and its promise of power? What could he use to help the clans thwart Gul'dan and take down the mighty pit lord? In early storyboards, Garrosh brought back different weapons from Azeroth, such as a gauntlet that gave him otherworldly strength. But in the end, the team settled on something else that would be featured in the game.

Collaborating with the game team, cinematics found their answer in a weapon that was being developed for use in *Mists of Pandaria*'s final chapter: the iron star, a spiked, mobile siege engine filled with explosives. Garrosh wouldn't bring a physical weapon to Draenor, but a concept of one and the knowledge of how to build it. This technology would become integral to the formation of the Iron Horde—the new coalition of uncorrupted orcs led by Grommash Hellscream but orchestrated by Garrosh as his latest attempt at creating his ideal Horde.

OPPOSITE
Storyboard frames show Grommash aiming the iron star at Mannoroth.

THIS PAGE
Designs for the iron star from the game team detail the weapon's inner workings.

MECHANICAL THEORY

WITH JUST TWO YEARS TO BUILD AN ARMY, MECHANIZATION LIMITED TO ONE MAIN ADVANCEMENT: THE COAL-FIRED CENTRIFUGAL ENGINE, (AN EARLY VERSION SEEN IN 5.4)

COAL FUELED
ENGINE
CAN SPIN
OR
AXIS CAN
SPIN

FIXED, TURNS AXLE TO DRIVE CHAIN

SPIKED VERSION CAN ROLL BY ITSELF

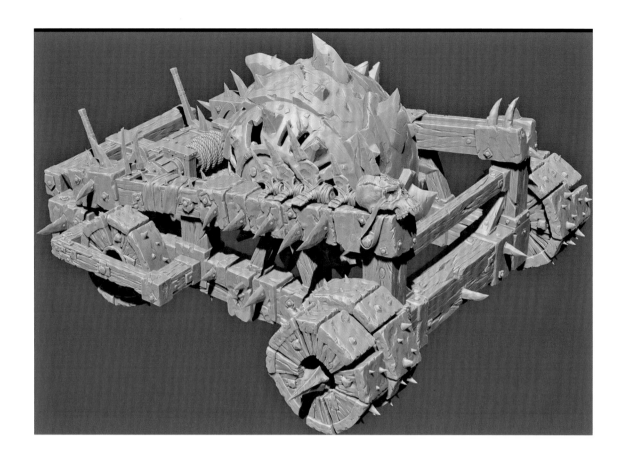

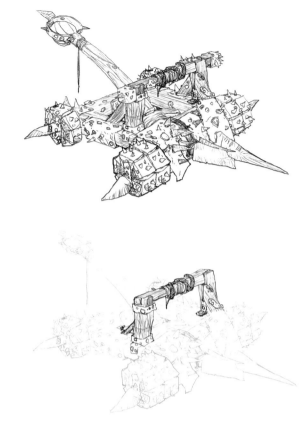

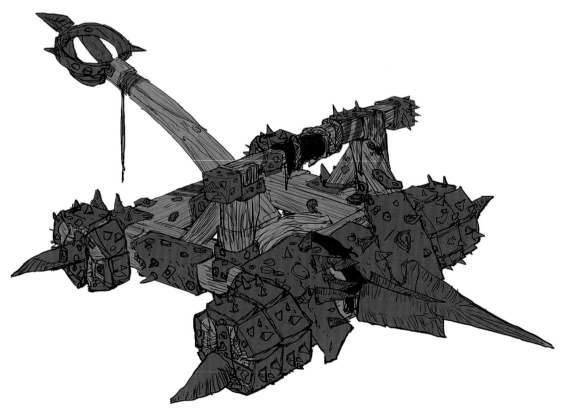

ABOVE AND LEFT
Designs for the catapults used against Mannoroth.

OPPOSITE AND TOP LEFT
The orcs first attempt to chain the pit lord with harpoons before unleashing the iron star, so artists developed a design that would serve dual purposes and stay compact enough for Grommash to move it alone.

THE THRONE
OF KIL'JAEDEN

THE BACKDROP FOR THE CINEMATIC IS TH⸱ Throne of Kil'jaeden, a mountain peak named after on⸱ of the Burning Legion's demonic commanders. It's ⸱ moonlit night, and lighting the scene required carefu⸱ planning. There are three main color tones that th⸱ team sought to highlight in the cinematic: the blue ligh⸱ of the moon, the fiery reds and oranges of the torche⸱ carried by the army of orcs, and the bright glowing gree⸱ of the blood pools and Mannoroth himself. Carefu⸱ attention was paid to the color script to make sur⸱ the mood was right from shot to shot. No one colo⸱ oversaturated any frame, and only two of the three mai⸱ tones were highlighted in any frame. Mixing too man⸱ colors together would sabotage the mood, so the tear⸱ also made sure the color tones never touch—insteac⸱ the colors are broken up by shadow as character⸱ move in and out of the light. One of the main goals i⸱ maintaining the cinematic's ominous mood was to keep⸱ the characters in darkness as much as possible, usin⸱ just enough light to identify the character and what the⸱ are doing.

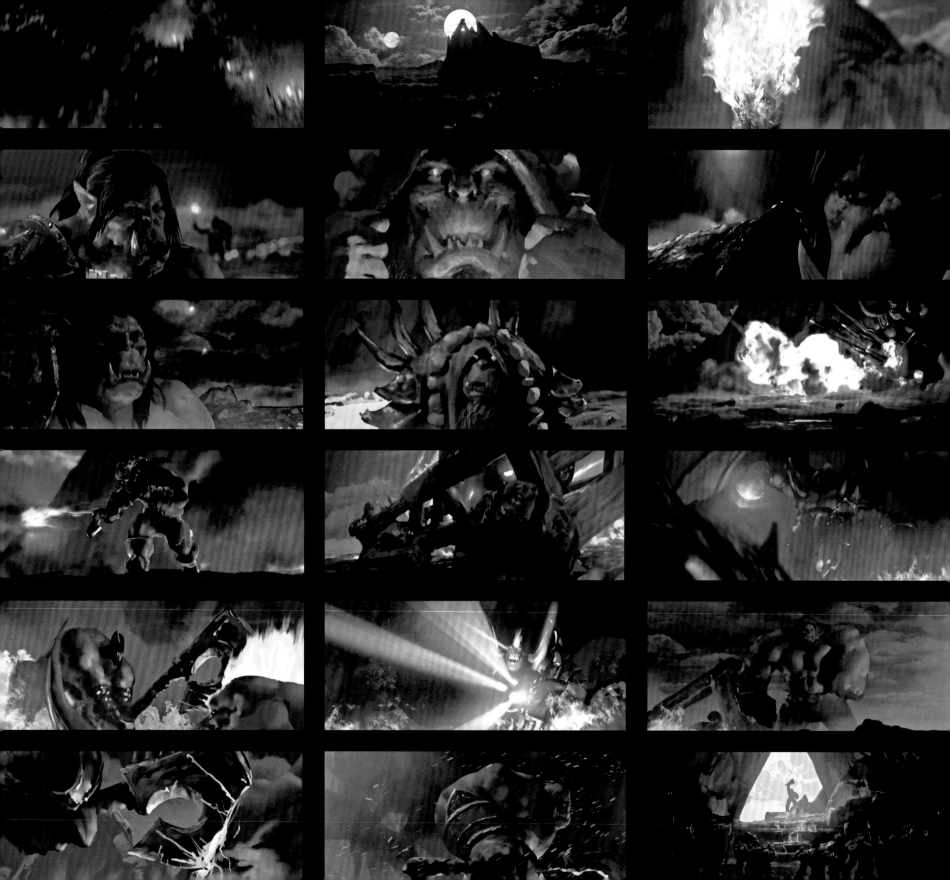

TOP
The Throne of Kil'jaeden, from sketch to render and final frame.

LEFT
Concept for the towering rock structures on the plateau.

RIGHT
Concept art envisions the Throne of Kil'jaeden in daylight.

BOTTOM
Concept art for the natural stone archways leading up to the peak and the path snaking up the mountain.

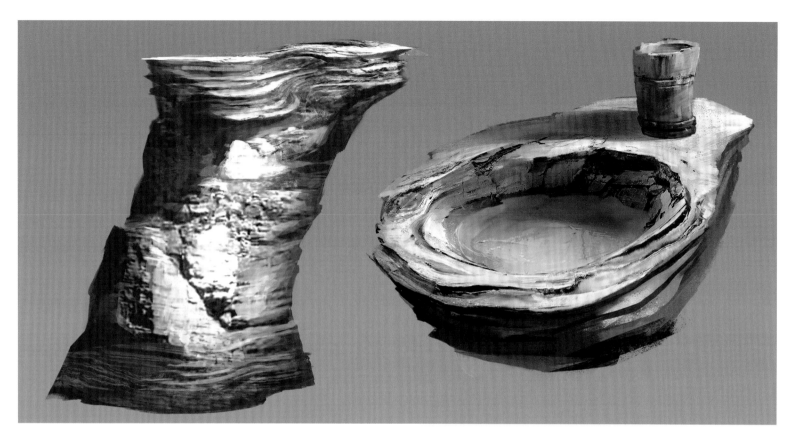

The team wanted the demon blood to feel evil and otherworldly, but also believable. Attention was paid to getting the right viscosity as the blood was poured and making sure that it smeared and stuck to the chalice.

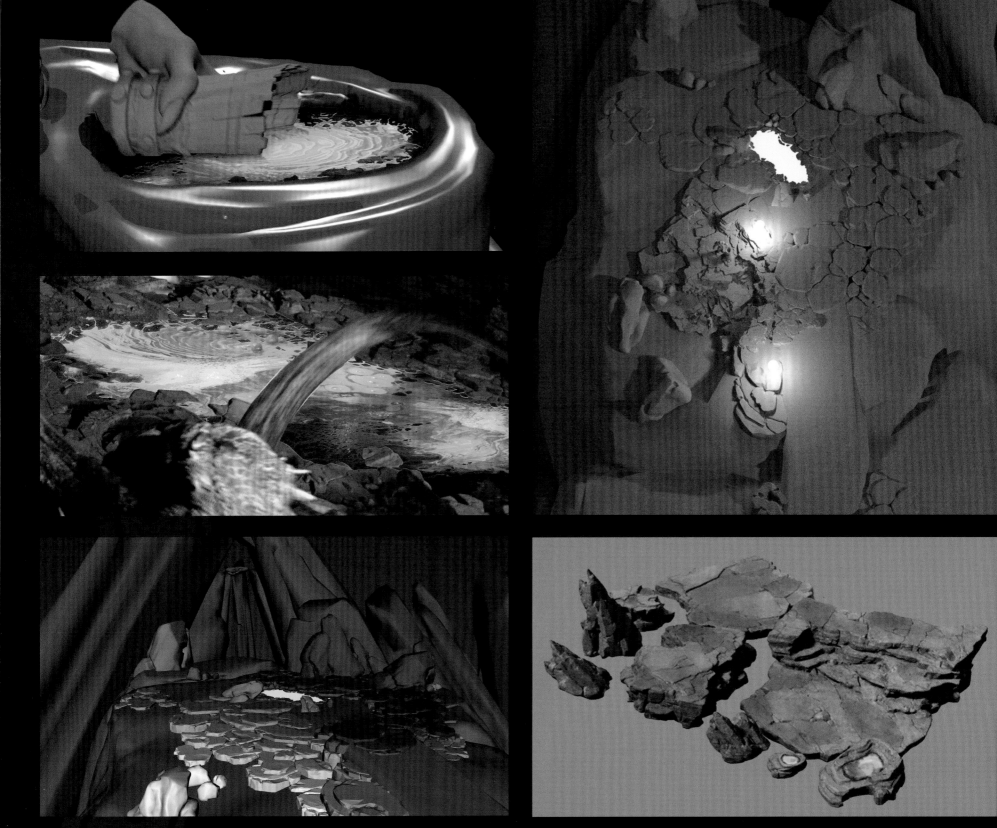

THE DARK PORTAL

"WE WILL NEVER BE SLAVES! BUT WE *WILL* BE CONQUERORS."

—GROMMASH HELLSCREAM

FEW PLACES IN WARCRAFT LORE ARE AS essential as the Dark Portal, the gateway that enabled the Horde's first invasion of Azeroth in *Warcraft: Orcs & Humans*. The portal had been long familiar to players who had experienced the *Burning Crusade* expansion. But the *Warlords of Draenor* cinematic ends with a shot of a new version of the Dark Portal under construction— this time by the Iron Horde.

The team thought of the portal itself as a character, with every element of the final shot planned to highlight the threat and menace it poses. Surrounded by shadow and lit at first only by the torches of the innumerable orcs constructing it, the Dark Portal is revealed to be massive, a warning that a powerful new enemy would soon invade Azeroth. Broad landscapes such as the one that the camera eventually settles on in showing the Dark Portal are very difficult to navigate for digital artists. Our eyes are adept at picking up on small details that appear fake when viewing a large-scale environment, so the shot required an enormous amount of detail and modeling to get the desired impact.

LORDS OF WAR

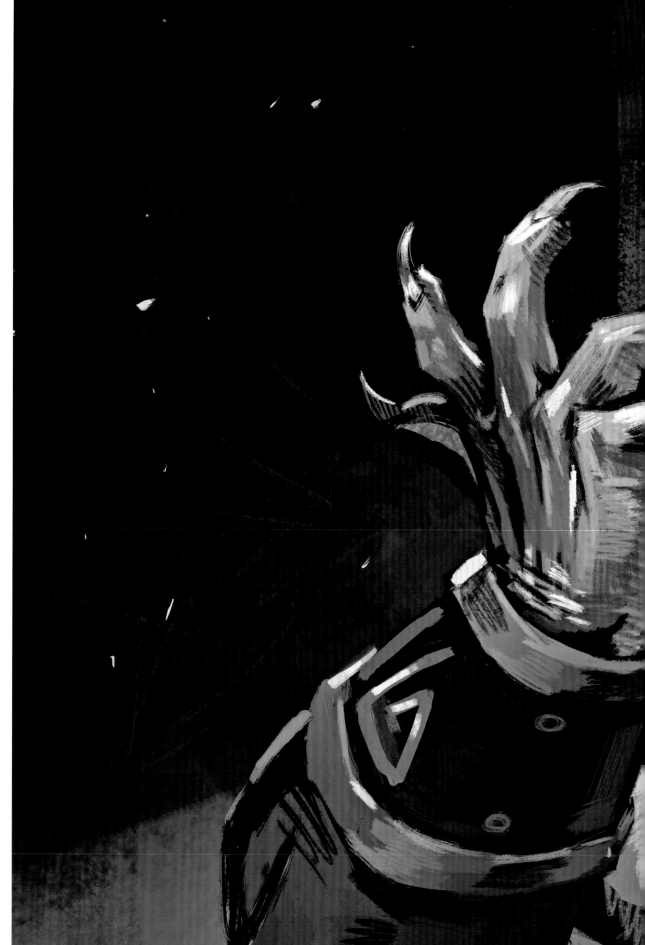

dark and brutal, meant to introduce players to some of
the main heroes and villains of *Warlords of Draenor*.
The first four episodes each center on a crucible event
in the life of the warlords, a formative act of murder,
revenge, or bloodlust that would help key players
into the psychology and background of the characters
they would encounter in the game. The final episode
gives us the backstory and motivations of the stories'
narrator, the draenei paladin Maraad, who saw his
people hunted to the verge of extinction by these
warlords a generation prior.

Telling these harsh origin stories required a vastly
different art style than the one used for *Burdens
of Shaohao*, *World of Warcraft*'s first motion-story
series. Inspired in part by film and noir comics, the
team zeroed in on a gritty, high-contrast look, with
exaggerated shadows; in fact, for a period of time, the
episodes were planned to be strictly black and white.
In addition, the team sought to push the characters'
anatomy into a more realistic place—the designs are still
highly stylized, with bulky shapes, but these are orcs like
viewers have never seen before.

KARGATH

BEFORE KARGATH WAS A WARLORD, HE was a slave and a gladiator fighting under the false promise that freedom awaited him should he kill one hundred orcs in the arena.

His bloody origin story was the first hint that *Lords of War* would explore darker themes. Finding the right balance of how much violence to show came about through experimentation. With Kargath, the team pushed the savagery of Draenor in a way many found unsettling. "You can show a dude chopping off his hand with a rock, and people will look at it and say, 'Yeah, what else you got?' We're immune to that level of violence," says Doug Gregory, who directed the cinematic. "But when I showed Kargath's fingernail peeling backwards as he tried to pry the rock from its perch? Let's just say I had to cut that shot a lot shorter."

"TAKE YOUR VENGEANCE."

—KARGATH BLADEFIST

THIS PAGE
Storyboards by Ted Boonthanakit culminate with a frame showing Kargath leading a force of orc gladiators with amputated hands against the ogres.

OPPOSITE
Originally intended to be in black and white, these paintings had color tones added to them later.

GROMMASH

GROMMASH HELLSCREAM WAS THE
leader of the Warsong clan and Garrosh Hellscream's
father. When it came time to tell the story of Grommash's
legendary will in *Lords of War*, the seed of the cinematic
was a single image: the chieftain, beaten, starved, and tied
to a tree. Impossibly, Grommash lures his ogre captor
with his whispers and takes his revenge.

Orcs are bulky and fierce. What does an emaciated orc
on the verge of death look like? It's not something that
had been explored much in Warcraft art previously. With
the challenge of depicting the Warsong chieftain in this
debilitated state, the team decided to keep Grommash's
ribcage oversized. "There's a big enormous guy in there,"
notes artist Laurel Austin, "but he's just wasted away."

"THIS WOLF STILL HAS TEETH."

—Grommash Hellscream

OPPOSITE TOP
The Warsong clan rallies to the banner of Grommash Hellscream.

OPPOSITE BOTTOM
Golka begs for a warrior's death.

RIGHT
Rough sketches that inspired the cinematic.

BELOW
Components from a final painting, ready to be animated.

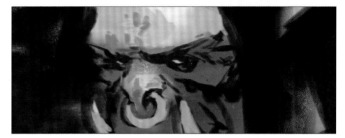

DUROTAN

DUROTAN, THE FUTURE LEADER OF THE FROSTWOLF clan, faced a dire choice as a youngling: leave his deathly ill mother behind, as his brother advised, or pay a heavy price to save her. While the cinematics team was able to use Durotan's detailed character model from the game as reference for illustrating him as an adult, much of the cinematic takes place while Durotan is much younger. In envisioning Durotan as an adolescent, artist Laurel Austin sought to retain elements from the in-game model but shrink them down. Young Durotan has a much slimmer figure, and his tusks will grow quite a bit yet.

"DUROTAN WORE STORMFANG'S FUR UNTIL THE END OF HIS DAYS . . . A REMINDER THAT EVEN THE MOST NOBLE OF ORCS MAY FALL PREY TO THE SAVAGERY WITHIN."

—MARAAD

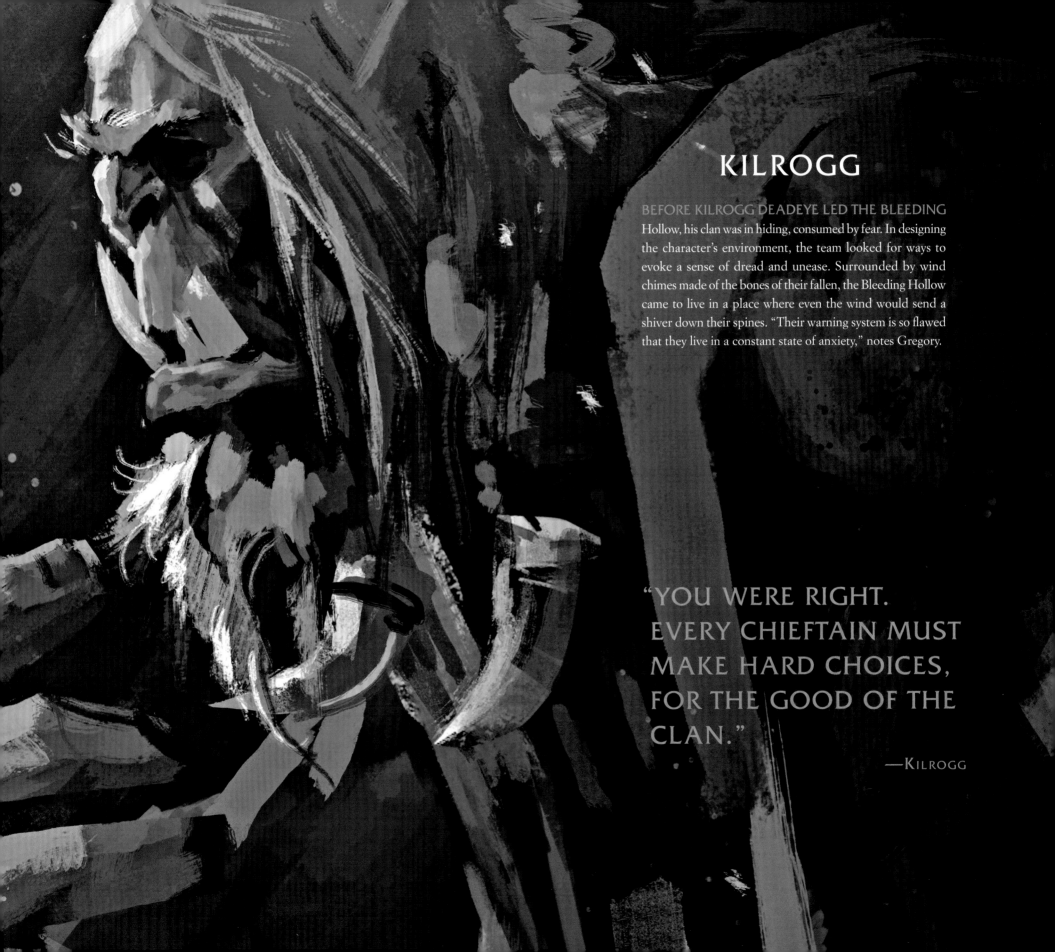

KILROGG

BEFORE KILROGG DEADEYE LED THE BLEEDING Hollow, his clan was in hiding, consumed by fear. In designing the character's environment, the team looked for ways to evoke a sense of dread and unease. Surrounded by wind chimes made of the bones of their fallen, the Bleeding Hollow came to live in a place where even the wind would send a shiver down their spines. "Their warning system is so flawed that they live in a constant state of anxiety," notes Gregory.

"YOU WERE RIGHT.
EVERY CHIEFTAIN MUST
MAKE HARD CHOICES,
FOR THE GOOD OF THE
CLAN."

—KILROGG

THE CINEMATIC ART OF **WORLD OF WARCRAFT**

MARAAD

VINDICATOR MARAAD BATTLED THE demonic orcs of the first Horde, and it's his impassioned voice that seeks to educate Varian Wrynn, leader of the Alliance, into acting to stop the Iron Horde from repeating their crimes, this time on Azeroth. He witnessed the slaughter of his people in Shattrath and is haunted by his failure to protect them.

PAGES 240–241
In order to bring glory to the Bleeding Hollow clan, Kilrogg must usurp his father.

THIS PAGE
The assault on Shattrath City by demon-corrupted orcs.

OPPOSITE
Maraad gathers the refugees to lead them away from the battle.

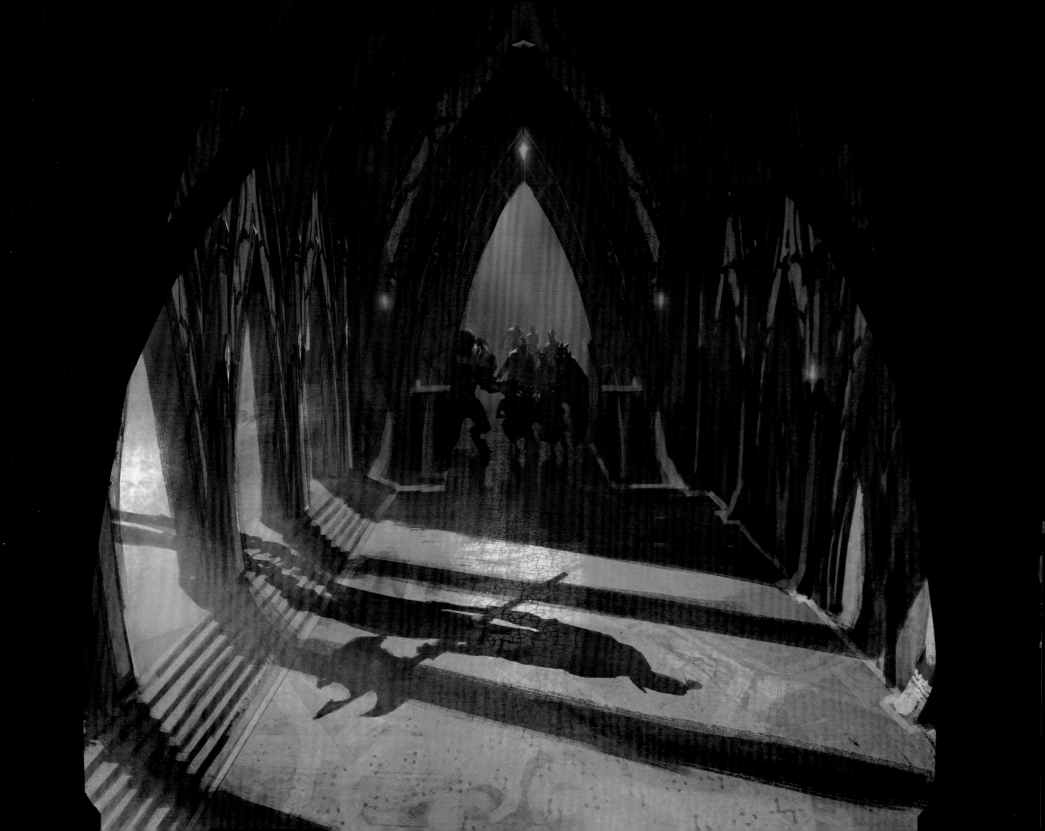

"THE LIGHT THAT I PROMISED WOULD BE WITH THEM HAD FORSAKEN THEM INSTEAD. JUST AS I HAD."

—Maraad

TITAN
BOOKS

Published by Titan Books, London, in 2019.

TITAN BOOKS
A division of Titan Publishing Group Ltd
144 Southwark Street
London SE1 0UP
www.titanbooks.com

Find us on Facebook: www.facebook.com/titanbooks
Follow us on Twitter: @TitanBooks

A CIP catalogue record for this title is available from the British Library.

ISBN: 9781789092981

FOR BLIZZARD ENTERTAINMENT

Written By: Greg Solano
Additional Writing: Matt Burns
Lead Editor: Greg Solano
Art Direction: Chris Thunig
Design: Evelyn Furuta
Game Team Direction: Alex Afrasiabi, Steve Aguilar, Ely Cannon, Steve Danuser, Jennifer Hauer, Ion Hazzikostas, Dusty Nolting, Marie Peters, Glenn Rane, Chris Robinson
Lore Consultation: Madi Buckingham, Sean Copeland, Christi Kugler, Justin Parker
Production: Allison Irons, Brianne M Loftis, Timothy Loughran, Paul Morrissey, Alix Nicholaeff, Derek Rosenberg, Cara Samuelsen
Director, Consumer Products: Byron Parnell
Directors, Creative Development: Ralph Sanchez and David Seeholzer
Special Thanks: Jeff Chamberlain, Steven Chen, Samwise Didier, Doug Gregory, Terran Gregory, Mike Hardison, Phillip Hillenbrand, James McCoy, Marc Messenger, Matt Samia, Justin Thavirat

Manufactured in China

10 9 8 7 6 5 4 3 2 1

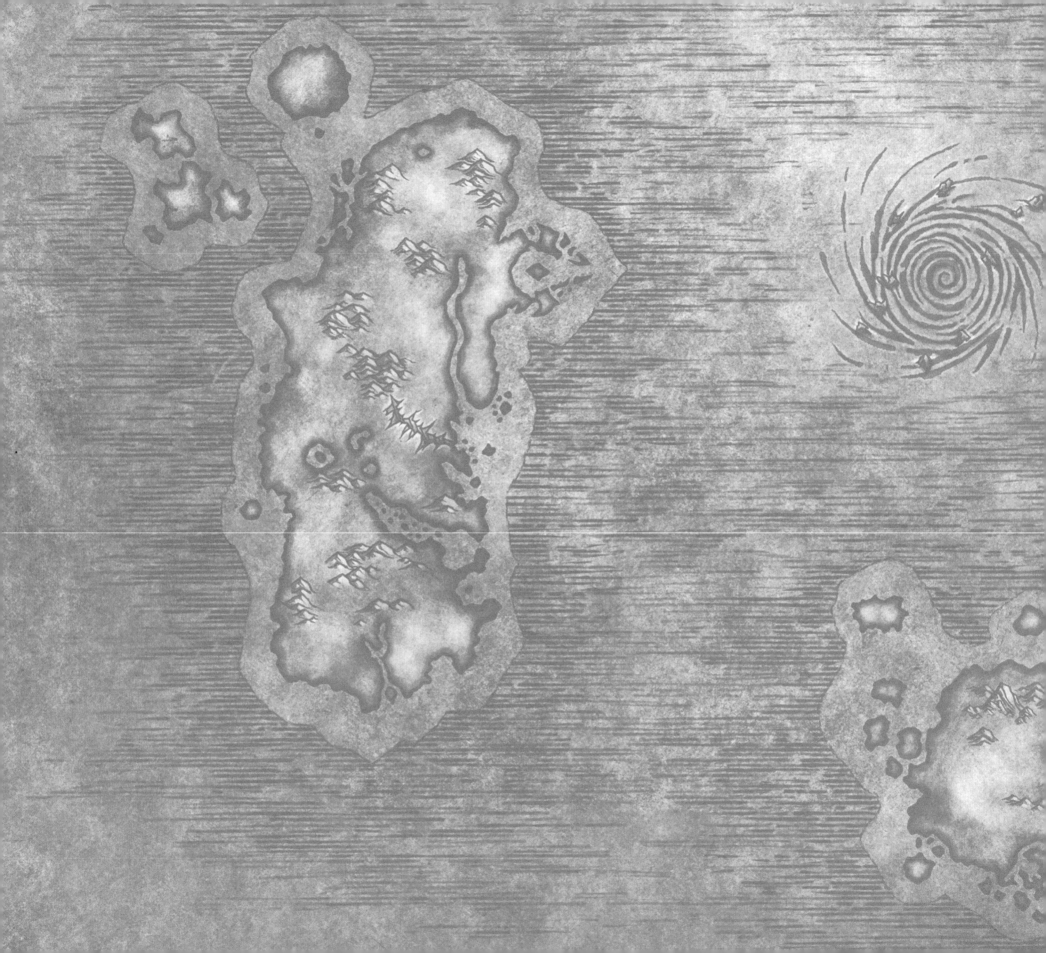